OLYMPIAD WORKBOOK

9

INTERNATIONAL ENGLISH OLYMPIAD

AF390084

01 Learning Objectives

02 Multiple Choice Questions

03 HOTS (Achievers Section)

04 Model Test Paper

05 Answer Keys and Solutions

06 OMR Answer Sheet

V&S PUBLISHERS

Published by:

V&S PUBLISHERS

F-2/16, Ansari road, Daryaganj, New Delhi-110002
☎ 23240026, 23240027 • *Fax:* 011-23240028
✉ info@vspublishers.com • 🌐 www.vspublishers.com

Online Brandstore: amazon.in/vspublishers

Regional Office : Hyderabad

5-1-707/1, Brij Bhawan (Beside Central Bank of India Lane)
Bank Street, Koti, Hyderabad - 500 095
☎ 040-24737290
✉ vspublishershyd@gmail.com

Follow us on:   

BUY OUR BOOKS FROM: AMAZON FLIPKART

© Copyright: *V&S* PUBLISHERS
ISBN 978-81-978021-0-2
New Edition

DISCLAIMER

PUBLISHER'S NOTE

V&S Publishers has carved a significant niche in the publishing industry over the last decade, having successfully published more than 1000 titles across 9 languages spanning over 50 subject categories. Being known for the quality of content, we have built a reputation of excellence and reliability. We have consistently delivered **"Value & Substance"** to our readers, through a wide range of titles across a variety of genres covering school books, fiction and non-fiction that caters to different people from every section of the society.

The **Olympiad Guidebooks for classes 1-10** across all subjects, launched almost a decade ago, under the **GEN X Imprint**, became a go-to-source for the school students in no time, owing to their invaluable and substantive content written in a guidebook pattern,.

Having successfully sold a million copies of the same and in response to demand by both students as well as shopkeepers nationwide; we now present before you our newly launched **Olympiad Workbook Series**, designed for **classes 1-10 across 4 subjects**.

The workbooks are meticulously curated by a team of experienced educators, researchers and subject matter experts, edited by professionals and peer reviewed by teachers. The team has poured its efforts and expertise into creating a crisp and concise workbook which will help and guide the students to the path of success in Olympiad exams. The **MCQs** identified will not only help in scoring top marks in Olympiads but also inculcate a sense of deeper understanding of the subject, by way of solving **HOTS** and referring to complete solutions at the end of the book.

Here we present our new release– **OLYMPIAD WORKBOOK (IEO) CLASS–9** having following features:

☞ Based on the latest syllabi
☞ MCQs with comprehensive coverage of topics
☞ HOTS Questions liberally included
☞ A dedicated chapter on logical reasoning
☞ Model test paper for thorough practice
☞ Sample OMR sheet for real time simulation

We have made sure through our best efforts, that this workbook strictly follows the latest syllabi and patterns of the Olympiad Examination.

As **V&S Publishers** continuously strive to enhance the readability and maintain the credibility of our academic publications, we seek the support of our valuable readers in influencing and enriching the lives of future generations of students.

P.S. While every care has been taken to ensure the correctness of the content, if you come across any error, howsoever minor, do not hesitate to discuss with teachers while pointing that out to us in no uncertain terms.

We wish you all the best for your exams!

DISTINCTIVE FEATURES

01 — Learning Objectives

They list the whole chapter as subtopics, helping the teachers to guide children in a step-by-step manner.

02 — Multiple Choice Questions

MCQs act as an excellent learning aid, helping you to understand and work on your mistakes.

03 — HOTS (Achievers Section)

The High Order Thinking Questions aim to help the student to solve Application-based questions and gain practical understanding of the subject.

04 — Model Test Paper

Model test paper are provided at the end of each book, which help the student to test the knowledge which they have gained after thorough reading of all chapters.

05 — Answer Key

Detailed Answer Key along with explanations aid the pupil to indentify, understand the mistakes they make during the course of Olympiad preparation.

CONTENTS

SYNONYMS, ANTONYMS, HOMOPHONES AND HOMONYMS

LEARNING OBJECTIVES

➤ Concept of Synonym and Antonym

PRACTICE EXERCISE

I. Choose the correct synonym of the underlined word from the options.

1. I am <u>terrible</u> at mathematics.
    (A) good   (B) awful
    (C) brilliant   (D) none of these

2. I found several spelling <u>mistakes</u>.
    (A) errors   (B) corrections
    (C) difficult   (D) none of these

3. Mr. Singh <u>required</u> five visas made for the family trip for abroad.
    (A) took   (B) wanted
    (C) needed   (D) none of these

4. He tried to <u>remember</u> a poem.
    (A) write   (B) rewrite
    (C) recollect   (D) none of these

5. He used <u>unlawful</u> methods to become rich.
    (A) illegal   (B) right
    (C) roundabout   (D) none of these

6. Kings are always associated with <u>courage</u>.
    (A) nobility
    (B) bravery
    (C) riches
    (D) none of these

7. Rita was <u>content</u> only after she got her ice-cream.
    (A) happy   (B) satisfied
    (C) quiet   (D) none of these

8. His <u>statement</u> accounted to slander.
    (A) truth   (B) lies
    (C) libel   (D) none of these

9. Non-biodegradable matter is <u>useless</u> in this day and age.
    (A) worthless   (B) useful
    (C) annoying   (D) none of these

10. It was <u>forbidden</u> to go into the forest.
    (A) fine   (B) un-allowed
    (C) prohibited   (D) none of these

II. Directions: Pick out the nearest correct meaning or synonym of the word given is capital letters.

11. GERMINATE
    (A) decay   (B) breed
    (C) produce   (D) sprout

12. EFFICACY
    (A) delicacy
    (B) ruthlessness
    (C) efficiency
    (D) solemnity

13. MAGNATE
    (A) tycoon
    (B) senior executive
    (C) non-magnetic
    (D) symbolic
14. FACET
    (A) sweet
    (B) tap
    (C) deceit
    (D) aspect
15. PERNICIOUS
    (A) deadly
    (B) curious
    (C) gorgeous
    (D) expensive
16. PERSUADE
    (A) assure   (B) opinionated
    (C) convince   (D) cheat
17. FORTIFY
    (A) topple   (B) destroy
    (C) reproduce   (D) strengthen
18. PHENOMENAL
    (A) incidental   (B) eventful
    (C) natural   (D) extraordinary
19. PARADIGM
    (A) solution   (B) model
    (C) discovery   (D) invention
20. HONORARY
    (A) honest   (B) dignified
    (C) unpaid   (D) praiseworthy
21. FACULTY
    (A) privilege   (B) desire
    (C) branch   (D) ability
22. FORESEE
    (A) contemplate   (B) visualise
    (C) assume   (D) hypothesis

23. ANNEX
    (A) add   (B) low
    (C) copy   (D) initial
24. MENAGE
    (A) suffocation
    (B) system
    (C) law
    (D) household
25. DILEMMA
    (A) darkness
    (B) freedom
    (C) trap
    (D) confusion
26. RIGMAROLE
    (A) short-cut
    (B) lengthy procedure
    (C) unnecessary burden
    (D) happy responsibility
27. TRANSCEND
    (A) lower
    (B) climb
    (C) energise
    (D) cross
28. IMPERATIVE
    (A) order
    (B) command
    (C) suggestion
    (D) necessity
29. EXEMPT
    (A) duty
    (B) provide
    (C) relieve of
    (D) forgive
30. INFIRMITY
    (A) disease
    (B) malady
    (C) weakness
    (D) slimness

I. Directions: Pick out the nearest correct meaning or synonym of the word given is capital letters.

31. BAFFLE

(A) insult
(B) frustrate
(C) defame
(D) antagonise

32. DAUNT

(A) detain
(B) annoy
(C) abuse
(D) intimidate

33. BEHOLDEN

(A) upright
(B) lovable
(C) grateful
(D) obliged

34. SOLICIT

(A) beseech
(B) require
(C) claim
(D) demand

35. CLUMSY

(A) adroit
(B) dexterous
(C) rough
(D) ungraceful

Darken Your Choice with HB Pencil

1. Ⓐ Ⓑ Ⓒ Ⓓ	8. Ⓐ Ⓑ Ⓒ Ⓓ	15. Ⓐ Ⓑ Ⓒ Ⓓ	22. Ⓐ Ⓑ Ⓒ Ⓓ	29. Ⓐ Ⓑ Ⓒ Ⓓ
2. Ⓐ Ⓑ Ⓒ Ⓓ	9. Ⓐ Ⓑ Ⓒ Ⓓ	16. Ⓐ Ⓑ Ⓒ Ⓓ	23. Ⓐ Ⓑ Ⓒ Ⓓ	30. Ⓐ Ⓑ Ⓒ Ⓓ
3. Ⓐ Ⓑ Ⓒ Ⓓ	10. Ⓐ Ⓑ Ⓒ Ⓓ	17. Ⓐ Ⓑ Ⓒ Ⓓ	24. Ⓐ Ⓑ Ⓒ Ⓓ	31. Ⓐ Ⓑ Ⓒ Ⓓ
4. Ⓐ Ⓑ Ⓒ Ⓓ	11. Ⓐ Ⓑ Ⓒ Ⓓ	18. Ⓐ Ⓑ Ⓒ Ⓓ	25. Ⓐ Ⓑ Ⓒ Ⓓ	32. Ⓐ Ⓑ Ⓒ Ⓓ
5. Ⓐ Ⓑ Ⓒ Ⓓ	12. Ⓐ Ⓑ Ⓒ Ⓓ	19. Ⓐ Ⓑ Ⓒ Ⓓ	26. Ⓐ Ⓑ Ⓒ Ⓓ	33. Ⓐ Ⓑ Ⓒ Ⓓ
6. Ⓐ Ⓑ Ⓒ Ⓓ	13. Ⓐ Ⓑ Ⓒ Ⓓ	20. Ⓐ Ⓑ Ⓒ Ⓓ	27. Ⓐ Ⓑ Ⓒ Ⓓ	34. Ⓐ Ⓑ Ⓒ Ⓓ
7. Ⓐ Ⓑ Ⓒ Ⓓ	14. Ⓐ Ⓑ Ⓒ Ⓓ	21. Ⓐ Ⓑ Ⓒ Ⓓ	28. Ⓐ Ⓑ Ⓒ Ⓓ	35. Ⓐ Ⓑ Ⓒ Ⓓ

SPELLING, COLLOCATIONS AND JUMBLED WORDS

PRACTICE EXERCISE

I. Choose the correct spelling.

1. (A) buy   (B) buye
    (C) boy   (D) none of these

2. (A) money   (B) mony
    (A) maney   (D) none of these

3. (A) schoul   (B) school
    (C) schaul   (D) none of these

4. (A) about   (B) abowt
    (C) aboat   (D) none of these

5. (A) rane   (B) rain
    (C) rene   (D) none of these

6. (A) right   (B) righte
    (C) reght   (D) none of these

7. (A) houer   (B) hour
    (C) hoar   (D) none of these

8. (A) doctor   (B) docter
    (C) doctar   (D) none of these

9. (A) deep   (B) diep
    (C) daep   (D) none of these

10. (A) nonne   (B) none
    (C) noene   (D) none of these

11. (A) dependant   (B) dependent
    (C) depandent   (D) none of these

12. (A) biased   (B) biassed
    (C) biesed   (D) none of these

13. (A) cafateria   (B) cafeteria
    (C) cefatria   (D) none of these

14. (A) autumn   (B) autunm
    (C) autamn   (D) none of these

15. (A) embarrass   (B) embarass
    (C) embaress   (D) none of these

16. (A) enviroment   (B) environment
    (C) envirament   (D) none of these

17. (A) censor   (B) censer
    (C) cansor   (D) none of these

18. (A) labratory   (B) laboratory
    (C) lebratory   (D) none of these

19. (A) skying   (B) skiing
    (C) skyeng   (D) none of these

20. (A) controlled   (B) controled
    (C) contalled   (D) none of these

II. Find the correctly spelt word from the given options.

21. (A) Treachrous   (B) Trecherous
    (C) Trechearous   (D) Treacherous

22. (A) Forcast   (B) Forecaste
    (C) Forcaust   (D) Forecast

23. (A) Rigerous   (B) Rigourous
    (C) Regerous   (D) Rigorous

24. (A) Palete   (B) Palet
    (C) Palatte   (D) Pelate
25. (A) Bouquete   (B) Bouquette
    (C) Bouquet   (D) Boqquet
26. (A) Itinarery   (B) Itinerary
    (C) Itenary   (D) Itinarary
27. (A) Survaillance   (B) Surveillance
    (C) Survellance   (D) Surveilance

28. (A) Sepulchral   (B) Sepilchrle
    (C) Sepalchrul   (D) Sepalchrl
29. (A) Acommodation   (B) Accomodaton
    (C) Accommodation   (D) Acomodation
30. (A) Faithfuly   (B) Sincerely
    (C) Truely   (D) Affectionatly

HOTS (ACHIEVERS SECTION)

I. Fill in the blanks with the correct collocation/option.

31. My grandfather was a _______ smoker, so few people were surprised when he died of oral cancer.
    (A) serial   (B) heavy
    (C) big   (D) none of these
32. She was a _______ wife who loved her husband more than anything else in the whole universe.
    (A) devoted   (B) sincere
    (C) intelligent   (D) none of these

33. I always avoid his company because he is a terrible _______.
    (A) bore   (B) nuisance
    (C) guy   (D) none of these
34. It is a golden _______ if you miss it, you will regret it.
    (A) chance   (B) opportunity
    (C) offer   (D) none of these
35. She seemed quite interested in buying that house, but at the last moment, she changed her _______.
    (A) mind   (B) thoughts
    (C) offer   (D) none of these

—Darken Your Choice with HB Pencil—

1. Ⓐ Ⓑ Ⓒ Ⓓ	8. Ⓐ Ⓑ Ⓒ Ⓓ	15. Ⓐ Ⓑ Ⓒ Ⓓ	22. Ⓐ Ⓑ Ⓒ Ⓓ	29. Ⓐ Ⓑ Ⓒ Ⓓ
2. Ⓐ Ⓑ Ⓒ Ⓓ	9. Ⓐ Ⓑ Ⓒ Ⓓ	16. Ⓐ Ⓑ Ⓒ Ⓓ	23. Ⓐ Ⓑ Ⓒ Ⓓ	30. Ⓐ Ⓑ Ⓒ Ⓓ
3. Ⓐ Ⓑ Ⓒ Ⓓ	10. Ⓐ Ⓑ Ⓒ Ⓓ	17. Ⓐ Ⓑ Ⓒ Ⓓ	24. Ⓐ Ⓑ Ⓒ Ⓓ	31. Ⓐ Ⓑ Ⓒ Ⓓ
4. Ⓐ Ⓑ Ⓒ Ⓓ	11. Ⓐ Ⓑ Ⓒ Ⓓ	18. Ⓐ Ⓑ Ⓒ Ⓓ	25. Ⓐ Ⓑ Ⓒ Ⓓ	32. Ⓐ Ⓑ Ⓒ Ⓓ
5. Ⓐ Ⓑ Ⓒ Ⓓ	12. Ⓐ Ⓑ Ⓒ Ⓓ	19. Ⓐ Ⓑ Ⓒ Ⓓ	26. Ⓐ Ⓑ Ⓒ Ⓓ	33. Ⓐ Ⓑ Ⓒ Ⓓ
6. Ⓐ Ⓑ Ⓒ Ⓓ	13. Ⓐ Ⓑ Ⓒ Ⓓ	20. Ⓐ Ⓑ Ⓒ Ⓓ	27. Ⓐ Ⓑ Ⓒ Ⓓ	34. Ⓐ Ⓑ Ⓒ Ⓓ
7. Ⓐ Ⓑ Ⓒ Ⓓ	14. Ⓐ Ⓑ Ⓒ Ⓓ	21. Ⓐ Ⓑ Ⓒ Ⓓ	28. Ⓐ Ⓑ Ⓒ Ⓓ	35. Ⓐ Ⓑ Ⓒ Ⓓ

ANALOGY AND ONE WORD

LEARNING OBJECTIVES

➤ Analogy and its types
➤ Concept and usage of One Words

PRACTICE EXERCISE

I. Choose the correct option to draw analogy.

1. Paw : Cat :: Hoof : ?
   (A) Lamb
   (B) Elephant
   (C) Horse
   (d) None of these

2. Peacock : India :: Bear : ?
   (A) Australia
   (B) America
   (C) Russia
   (d) None of these

3. Flow : River :: Stagnant : ?
   (A) Rain
   (B) Stream
   (C) Pool
   (d) None of these

4. NATION : ANTINO :: HUNGRY : ?
   (A) HNUGRY
   (B) UHNGYR
   (C) YRNGUH
   (d) None of these

5. Architect : Building :: Sculptor : ?
   (A) Museum
   (B) Stone
   (C) Statue
   (d) None of these

6. Microphone : Loud :: Microscope : ?
   (A) Elongate
   (B) Investigate
   (C) Examine
   (d) None of these

7. Country : President :: State : ?
   (A) Governor
   (B) M.P
   (C) Legislator
   (d) None of these

8. Tree : Forest :: Grass : ?
   (A) Road
   (B) pool
   (C) Park
   (d) None of these

9. Peace : Chaos :: Creation : ?
   (A) Build
   (B) Construction
   (C) Destruction
   (d) None of these

10. Race : Fatigue :: Fast : ?
    (A) Food
    (B) Laziness
    (C) Hunger
    (d) None of these

II. **See the given analogy and state whether it is True or False.**

11. Effect/cause
Sharp : Blunt :: Sweet : Sour (True, False)

12. Antonyms
Sharp : Blunt :: Sweet : Sour (True, False)

13. Action/subject performing action
Kick : Ball :: Texting : Cell phone
(True, False)

14. Whole / part
Fire : Heat :: Study : Good grades
(True, False)

15. Synonyms
Strong : Sturdy :: Dry : Wet (True, False)

III. **Choose the correct option for the given group of words/phrases:**

16. A person who has prejudiced views.
(A) Bigot
(B) Bold
(C) Brave
(D) None of these

17. Something which leads or ends with death.
(A) Fatal
(B) fated
(C) Fat
(D) None of these

18. Only eats plants- normally used for animals
(A) Omnivorous
(B) Carnivorous
(C) Herbivorous
(D) None of these

19. Anything to do with the moon
(A) Lunatic
(B) Lunar
(C) Moon
(D) None of these

20. A person of a different nationality settling down in a new country.
(A) Immigrant
(B) Imminent
(C) Eminent
(D) None of these

21. All kinds of animals living in a particular place
(A) Plants
(B) Fauna
(C) Flora
(D) None of these

22. A follower of a leader–political or religious
(A) Discipline
(B) Disciple
(C) Follower
(D) None of these

23. A person who is qualified for a post or college or scholarship
(A) Eligible (B) Illegal
(C) Able (D) None of these

24. A school for little children or a room in the house for a newborn.
(A) Primary (B) Secondary
(C) Nursery (D) None of these

25. Almost see through
(A) Transparent (B) Opaque
(C) Clear (D) None of these

26. A house where parentless children are brought up.
(A) Orphan (B) Orphanage
(C) School (D) None of these

27. A professional rider in horse races
(A) Jockey (B) Horse Rider
(C) Jacky (D) None of these

28. A group of judges
(A) Jerry (B) Jury
(C) Judicial (D) None of these

29. A person who can use both right and left hand
(A) Ambidextrous (B) Amber
(C) Amorous (D) None of these

30. Dry weather with no rainfall
(A) Dry (B) Heat
(C) Drought (D) None of these

I. Find out the correct option to establish the relationship as shown in the given expression.

31. 'Dress' is related to 'Body' in the same way as 'Bangles' is related to:

    (A) Glass   (B) Lady

    (C) Wrist   (D) Beauty

32. Flower' is related to 'Bud' in the same way as 'Fruit' is related to:

    (A) Seed   (B) Tree

    (C) Flower   (D) Stem

33. 'Jackal' is related to 'Howl' in the same way as 'Cow' is related to:

    (A) Caws   (B) Hoot

    (C) Coo   (D) Moo

34. 'Smoke' is related to 'Pollution' in the same way as 'War' is related to:

    (A) Victory   (B) Treaty

    (C) Defeat   (D) Destruction

35. 'Rabbit' is related to 'Burrow' in the same way as 'Lunatic' is related to:

    (A) Prison   (b). Cell

    (C) Barrack   (D) Asylum

Darken Your Choice with HB Pencil

1. Ⓐ Ⓑ Ⓒ Ⓓ	8. Ⓐ Ⓑ Ⓒ Ⓓ	15. Ⓐ Ⓑ Ⓒ Ⓓ	22. Ⓐ Ⓑ Ⓒ Ⓓ	29. Ⓐ Ⓑ Ⓒ Ⓓ
2. Ⓐ Ⓑ Ⓒ Ⓓ	9. Ⓐ Ⓑ Ⓒ Ⓓ	16. Ⓐ Ⓑ Ⓒ Ⓓ	23. Ⓐ Ⓑ Ⓒ Ⓓ	30. Ⓐ Ⓑ Ⓒ Ⓓ
3. Ⓐ Ⓑ Ⓒ Ⓓ	10. Ⓐ Ⓑ Ⓒ Ⓓ	17. Ⓐ Ⓑ Ⓒ Ⓓ	24. Ⓐ Ⓑ Ⓒ Ⓓ	31. Ⓐ Ⓑ Ⓒ Ⓓ
4. Ⓐ Ⓑ Ⓒ Ⓓ	11. Ⓐ Ⓑ Ⓒ Ⓓ	18. Ⓐ Ⓑ Ⓒ Ⓓ	25. Ⓐ Ⓑ Ⓒ Ⓓ	32. Ⓐ Ⓑ Ⓒ Ⓓ
5. Ⓐ Ⓑ Ⓒ Ⓓ	12. Ⓐ Ⓑ Ⓒ Ⓓ	19. Ⓐ Ⓑ Ⓒ Ⓓ	26. Ⓐ Ⓑ Ⓒ Ⓓ	33. Ⓐ Ⓑ Ⓒ Ⓓ
6. Ⓐ Ⓑ Ⓒ Ⓓ	13. Ⓐ Ⓑ Ⓒ Ⓓ	20. Ⓐ Ⓑ Ⓒ Ⓓ	27. Ⓐ Ⓑ Ⓒ Ⓓ	34. Ⓐ Ⓑ Ⓒ Ⓓ
7. Ⓐ Ⓑ Ⓒ Ⓓ	14. Ⓐ Ⓑ Ⓒ Ⓓ	21. Ⓐ Ⓑ Ⓒ Ⓓ	28. Ⓐ Ⓑ Ⓒ Ⓓ	35. Ⓐ Ⓑ Ⓒ Ⓓ

PHRASAL VERBS AND IDIOMS 

4

➤ Concept of Phrasal Verbs
➤ Types of Phrasal Verbs
➤ Some common Idioms and their meanings

PRACTICE EXERCISE

I. Choose the correct phrasal verb in the following questions.

1. Could you turn _____ the TV? The soap opera is about to start.
   (A) back   (B) on
   (C) off   (D) out

2. There was nothing good on TV so I turned it _____ and went to bed.
   (A) off   (B) up
   (C) in   (D) down

3. The TV is too loud. Can you turn it _____ a bit?
   (A) up   (B) out
   (C) off   (D) down

4. The TV is too quiet. Can you turn it _____ a bit?
   (A) back   (B) off
   (C) up   (D) over

5. I've been looking _____ my car keys for half an hour. Have you seen them anywhere?
   (A) up   (B) for
   (C) after   (D) at

6. My mother has offered to look _____ the children, so we can go to the party.
   (A) for   (B) into
   (C) at   (D) after

7. If you don't know what the word means, you'll have to look it _____ in the dictionary.
   (A) for   (B) up
   (C) out   (D) off

8. The meeting has been put _____ to Friday as so many people have got the flu.
   (A) up   (B) in
   (C) back   (D) out

9. The meeting has been brought _____ to Monday due to the seriousness of the situation.
   (A) on   (B) out
   (C) down   (D) forward

10. The company is taking _____ new workers to meet this projected demand.
    (A) at   (B) on
    (C) up   (D) over

11. Our alarm clock is set to go _____ at 6 a.m.
    (A) away   (B) up
    (C) out   (D) off

12. Gary asked Cynthia to marry him, but she turned him _______.
   (A) down   (B) without
   (C) across   (D) over

13. The emergency workers managed to put _______ the fire.
   (A) off   (B) out
   (C) down   (D) without

14. Everyone thought she was English, but she turned _______ to be Canadian.
   (A) up   (B) off
   (C) by   (D) out

15. The math teacher lets students chew gum in class, but the French teacher does not put _______ with it.
   (A) over   (B) out
   (C) up   (D) along

16. The university students want to do _______ with tuition, because they think education should be free.
   (A) away   (B) out
   (C) up   (D) off

17. Nelson is a creative liar who is always making _______ unusual excuses for not doing his work.
   (A) up   (B) across
   (C) away   (D) off

18. Paula always comes _______ as very sincere.
   (A) out   (B) along
   (C) across   (D) away

19. Tom and Carol often have heated arguments, but they always make _______ later.
   (A) down   (B) away
   (C) up   (D) along

20. We have to clean _______ the house before my parents arrive.
   (A) down   (B) away
   (C) without   (D) up

21. The police officer almost captured the criminals, but they managed to get _______.
   (A) without   (B) over
   (C) along   (D) away

22. I have come down with a cold, but I will get _______ it soon.
   (A) over   (B) up
   (C) without   (D) above

23. Robert was expected to arrive at 8 o'clock, but he didn't turn _______ until midnight.
   (A) out   (B) up
   (C) off   (D) with

24. Peter needs either to get a raise or to get a better job, because he can't get _______ on his current salary.
   (A) by   (B) out
   (C) in   (D) off

25. Manuela and Glenda didn't like each other at first, but now they get _______.
   (A) over   (B) across
   (C) away   (D) along

II. Fill in the blanks with phrasal verb taking one word from each group/box.

Get, give, look, put, stand, take, turn	After, on, off, out, up

26. I often use Wikipedia to_______ information.

27. If you want to _______a bus in Delhi, you will have to queue.

28. Can I ___the TV? I want to watch the weather forecast.

29. It is very hard to _____ smoking.

30. It is so dark over here, you can really _______your sunglasses now.

Choose the correct option for the given idiom.

31. To make ends meet
    (A) A short story
    (B) To earn enough to live
    (C) To skip classes
    (D) None of these
32. Bolt from the blue
    (A) Sudden shock
    (B) To lose a tight game
    (C) To ask for help
    (D) None of these
33. To burn the candle at both ends
    (A) To argue endlessly
    (B) Long power cut
    (C) To work long hours
    (D) None of these
34. To bury the hatchet
    (A) To end enmity
    (B) To hide stolen treasure
    (C) To overexert
    (D) None of these
35. To spill the beans
    (A) To reveal a secret
    (B) To eat clumsily
    (C) To get exhausted
    (D) None of these

—Darken Your Choice with HB Pencil—

1.	Ⓐ Ⓑ Ⓒ Ⓓ	8.	Ⓐ Ⓑ Ⓒ Ⓓ	15.	Ⓐ Ⓑ Ⓒ Ⓓ	22.	Ⓐ Ⓑ Ⓒ Ⓓ	29.	Ⓐ Ⓑ Ⓒ Ⓓ
2.	Ⓐ Ⓑ Ⓒ Ⓓ	9.	Ⓐ Ⓑ Ⓒ Ⓓ	16.	Ⓐ Ⓑ Ⓒ Ⓓ	23.	Ⓐ Ⓑ Ⓒ Ⓓ	30.	Ⓐ Ⓑ Ⓒ Ⓓ
3.	Ⓐ Ⓑ Ⓒ Ⓓ	10.	Ⓐ Ⓑ Ⓒ Ⓓ	17.	Ⓐ Ⓑ Ⓒ Ⓓ	24.	Ⓐ Ⓑ Ⓒ Ⓓ	31.	Ⓐ Ⓑ Ⓒ Ⓓ
4.	Ⓐ Ⓑ Ⓒ Ⓓ	11.	Ⓐ Ⓑ Ⓒ Ⓓ	18.	Ⓐ Ⓑ Ⓒ Ⓓ	25.	Ⓐ Ⓑ Ⓒ Ⓓ	32.	Ⓐ Ⓑ Ⓒ Ⓓ
5.	Ⓐ Ⓑ Ⓒ Ⓓ	12.	Ⓐ Ⓑ Ⓒ Ⓓ	19.	Ⓐ Ⓑ Ⓒ Ⓓ	26.	Ⓐ Ⓑ Ⓒ Ⓓ	33.	Ⓐ Ⓑ Ⓒ Ⓓ
6.	Ⓐ Ⓑ Ⓒ Ⓓ	13.	Ⓐ Ⓑ Ⓒ Ⓓ	20.	Ⓐ Ⓑ Ⓒ Ⓓ	27.	Ⓐ Ⓑ Ⓒ Ⓓ	34.	Ⓐ Ⓑ Ⓒ Ⓓ
7.	Ⓐ Ⓑ Ⓒ Ⓓ	14.	Ⓐ Ⓑ Ⓒ Ⓓ	21.	Ⓐ Ⓑ Ⓒ Ⓓ	28.	Ⓐ Ⓑ Ⓒ Ⓓ	35.	Ⓐ Ⓑ Ⓒ Ⓓ

QUESTION FORMS

LEARNING OBJECTIVES

➤ Types of Questions

PRACTICE EXERCISE

I. Name the type of questions in the following sentences.

1. Can you swim?
2. Did he go to work or to school?
3. Has your class finished?
4. Where is my pen?
5. Who did you visit?
6. Why didn't he go to work?
7. Shall we go to your place or mine?
8. When will Lucy arrive?
9. Who called here so late?
10. What do you think about the movie?

II. Write questions for these answers.

11. **Ans:** She is opening a present.

    Q: ________________________________

12. **Ans:** The boys are hiding under Anita's bed.

    Q: ________________________________

13. **Ans:** My sister prefers porridge for break-fast.

    Q: ________________________________

14. **Ans:** On Thursday Prasad has Sociology, History and Maths.

    Q: ________________________________

15. **Ans:** Yesterday Anil and Anu went to the swimming pool.

    Q: ________________________________

16. **Ans:** The plane is landing at the airport.

    Q: ________________________________

17. **Ans:** The phone is ringing

    Q: ________________________________

18. **Ans:** Chitra will have to stop

    Q: ________________________________

19. **Ans:** Ashima new bike costs Rs. 90,000.

    Q: ________________________________

20. **Ans:** The girl is walking along the beach.

    Q: ________________________________

I. Write the correct question for each answer.

21. Ans: My brother loves ice-cream for dessert.

    Q: _______________________________

22. Ans: On Tuesday, Prateek is going for a movie.

    Q: _______________________________

23. Ans: Yesterday, Anil and Anu left for Dehradun.

    Q: _______________________________

II. Select correct options (question tags) to fill the blanks.

24. They haven't come, __________?
    (A) Has they   (B) have they
    (C) had they   (D) haven't they

25. You are free, __________?
    (A) Were you   (B) weren't you
    (C) Aren't you   (D) are you

───── Darken Your Choice with HB Pencil ─────

	A B C D		A B C D		A B C D		A B C D		A B C D
1.	Ⓐ Ⓑ Ⓒ Ⓓ	6.	Ⓐ Ⓑ Ⓒ Ⓓ	11.	Ⓐ Ⓑ Ⓒ Ⓓ	16.	Ⓐ Ⓑ Ⓒ Ⓓ	21.	Ⓐ Ⓑ Ⓒ Ⓓ
2.	Ⓐ Ⓑ Ⓒ Ⓓ	7.	Ⓐ Ⓑ Ⓒ Ⓓ	12.	Ⓐ Ⓑ Ⓒ Ⓓ	17.	Ⓐ Ⓑ Ⓒ Ⓓ	22.	Ⓐ Ⓑ Ⓒ Ⓓ
3.	Ⓐ Ⓑ Ⓒ Ⓓ	8.	Ⓐ Ⓑ Ⓒ Ⓓ	13.	Ⓐ Ⓑ Ⓒ Ⓓ	18.	Ⓐ Ⓑ Ⓒ Ⓓ	23.	Ⓐ Ⓑ Ⓒ Ⓓ
4.	Ⓐ Ⓑ Ⓒ Ⓓ	9.	Ⓐ Ⓑ Ⓒ Ⓓ	14.	Ⓐ Ⓑ Ⓒ Ⓓ	19.	Ⓐ Ⓑ Ⓒ Ⓓ	24.	Ⓐ Ⓑ Ⓒ Ⓓ
5.	Ⓐ Ⓑ Ⓒ Ⓓ	10.	Ⓐ Ⓑ Ⓒ Ⓓ	15.	Ⓐ Ⓑ Ⓒ Ⓓ	20.	Ⓐ Ⓑ Ⓒ Ⓓ	25.	Ⓐ Ⓑ Ⓒ Ⓓ

VERBS, ADVERBS AND CONCORD

6

LEARNING OBJECTIVES

➤ Verbs and its different types
➤ Modal Auxiliaries

➤ Adverbs and its different kinds
➤ Uses of Adverbs

PRACTICE EXERCISE

IV. Choose the correct option to fill in the blanks with the correct form of verb.

1. I _______ tennis every Sunday morning.
   (A) playing (B) play
   (C) am playing (D) am play

2. Don't make so much noise. Sarika _____ to study for her ESL test!
   (A) try   (B) tries
   (C) tried (D) is trying

3. Manav _______ his teeth before breakfast every morning.
   (A) will cleaned (B) is cleaning
   (C) cleans (D) clean

4. Sorry, she can't come to the phone. She _______ a bath!
   (A) is having (B) having
   (C) have   (D) has

5. _______ many times every winter in Frankfurt.
   (A) It snows (B) It snowed
   (C) It is snowing (D) It is snow

6. How many students in your class _______ from Korea?
   (A) comes (B) come
   (C) came (D) are coming

7. Weather report: "It's seven o'clock in Frankfurt and _______."
   (A) there is snow (B) it`s snowing
   (C) it snows (D) it snowed

8. Babies _______ when they are hungry.
   (A) cry   (B) cries
   (C) cried (D) are crying

9. Jane: "What _______ in the evenings?"
   Mary: "Usually I watch TV or read a book."
   (A) you doing (B) you do
   (C) do you do (D) are you doing

10. Jane: "What _______?"
    Mary: "I'm trying to fix my calculator."
    (A) you doing (B) you do
    (C) do you do (D) are you doing

11. Jane _______ her blue jeans today, but usually she wears a skirt or a dress.
    (A) wears (B) wearing
    (C) wear (D) is wearing

12. I think I _______ a new calculator. This one does not work properly any more.
    (A) needs (B) needed
    (C) need (D) am needing

13. Sorry, you can't borrow my pencil. I _______ it myself.
    (A) was using   (B) using
    (C) use   (d) am using
14. At a school dance:
    Jane: " _______ yourself?"
    Mary: "Yes, I'm having a great time!"
    (A) You enjoying
    (B) Enjoy you
    (C) Do you enjoy
    (D) Are you enjoying
15. I've just finished reading a story called Dangerous Game. It's about a man who _______ his wife because he doesn't want to lose her.
    (A) kills   (B) killed
    (C) kill   (D) is killing
16. What time _______
    (A) the train leaves?
    (B) leaves the train?
    (C) is the train leaving?
    (D) does the train leave?
17. Jane: "Are you going to the dance on Friday?"
    Mary: "No, I'm not. I _______ school dances; they're loud, hot and crowded!"
    (A) not enjoy
    (B) don't enjoy
    (C) doesn't enjoy
    (D) am not enjoying
18. I _______ for my pen. Have you seen it?
    (A) will look   (B) looking
    (C) look   (D) am looking
19. You can keep my iPod if you like. I _______ it any more.
    (A) don't use   (B) doesn't use
    (C) didn't use   (D) am not using

20. The phone _______ Can you answer it, please?
    (A) rings   (B) ring
    (C) rang   (D) is ringing
21. Have you ever _______ abroad?
    (a) went   (b) been
    (C) to   (d) go
22. She's _______ a shower at the moment.
    (a) taken   (b) takes
    (C) take   (d) taking
23. I always _______ before bed.
    (a) read   (b) to read
    (c) reading   (D) is read
24. He will _______ you later.
    (a) to call   (b) calls
    (c) calling   (d) call
25. I don't know who _______ the chair.
    (A) breaking   (B) broke
    (C) breaks   (D) break
26. We've all been _______ about you.
    (A) thinking   (B) thought
    (C) thinks   (D) to think
27. Someone _______ moved my bag.
    (A) have   (B) having
    (C) has   (D) haves
28. We _______ playing cards all afternoon.
    (A) were   (B) was
    (C) is   (D) be
29. Those _______ the type I like.
    (A) isn't   (B) aren't
    (B) don't   (D) won't
30. James asked me _______ him.
    (A) emailed   (B) to email
    (C) emailing   (D) email

Choose the correct form of verb to fill in the blanks.

31. She __________ to live in the country.
    - (A) enjoys
    - (B) used
    - (C) is used
    - (D) None of these

32. Naina __________ to look for a job in New York.
    - (A) has decided
    - (B) is thinking
    - (C) had better
    - (D) None of these

33. The children __________ to tidy up their bedrooms.
    - (A) were made
    - (B) expect you
    - (C) are trying
    - (D) None of these

34. The owner of the shop __________ him to leave.
    - (A) stopped
    - (B) wanted
    - (C) hoped
    - (D) None of these

35. Her husband __________ to come home early.
    - (A) succeeded
    - (B) is looking forward
    - (C) reminded her

—Darken Your Choice with HB Pencil—

1.	Ⓐ Ⓑ Ⓒ Ⓓ	8.	Ⓐ Ⓑ Ⓒ Ⓓ	15.	Ⓐ Ⓑ Ⓒ Ⓓ	22.	Ⓐ Ⓑ Ⓒ Ⓓ	29.	Ⓐ Ⓑ Ⓒ Ⓓ
2.	Ⓐ Ⓑ Ⓒ Ⓓ	9.	Ⓐ Ⓑ Ⓒ Ⓓ	16.	Ⓐ Ⓑ Ⓒ Ⓓ	23.	Ⓐ Ⓑ Ⓒ Ⓓ	30.	Ⓐ Ⓑ Ⓒ Ⓓ
3.	Ⓐ Ⓑ Ⓒ Ⓓ	10.	Ⓐ Ⓑ Ⓒ Ⓓ	17.	Ⓐ Ⓑ Ⓒ Ⓓ	24.	Ⓐ Ⓑ Ⓒ Ⓓ	31.	Ⓐ Ⓑ Ⓒ Ⓓ
4.	Ⓐ Ⓑ Ⓒ Ⓓ	11.	Ⓐ Ⓑ Ⓒ Ⓓ	18.	Ⓐ Ⓑ Ⓒ Ⓓ	25.	Ⓐ Ⓑ Ⓒ Ⓓ	32.	Ⓐ Ⓑ Ⓒ Ⓓ
5.	Ⓐ Ⓑ Ⓒ Ⓓ	12.	Ⓐ Ⓑ Ⓒ Ⓓ	19.	Ⓐ Ⓑ Ⓒ Ⓓ	26.	Ⓐ Ⓑ Ⓒ Ⓓ	33.	Ⓐ Ⓑ Ⓒ Ⓓ
6.	Ⓐ Ⓑ Ⓒ Ⓓ	13.	Ⓐ Ⓑ Ⓒ Ⓓ	20.	Ⓐ Ⓑ Ⓒ Ⓓ	27.	Ⓐ Ⓑ Ⓒ Ⓓ	34.	Ⓐ Ⓑ Ⓒ Ⓓ
7.	Ⓐ Ⓑ Ⓒ Ⓓ	14.	Ⓐ Ⓑ Ⓒ Ⓓ	21.	Ⓐ Ⓑ Ⓒ Ⓓ	28.	Ⓐ Ⓑ Ⓒ Ⓓ	35.	Ⓐ Ⓑ Ⓒ Ⓓ

NOUNS AND PRONOUNS

LEARNING OBJECTIVES

- ➤ Kinds of Nouns
- ➤ Usage of Nouns
- ➤ Usage of Pronoun
- ➤ Functions of Nouns
- ➤ Pronoun and its Types

PRACTICE EXERCISE

I. Choose the correct option.

1. Which of the following is a collective noun?
   (A) Apple   (B) Writer
   (C) Choir   (D) Lily

2. Which of the following is a proper noun?
   (A) Sinjini   (B) Freedom
   (C) Love   (D) Capital

3. Which of the following is a common noun?
   (A) Iron   (B) London
   (C) Swarm   (D) Officer

4. Which of the following is an abstract noun?
   (A) Birds   (B) Greed
   (C) Clown   (D) Elephant

5. Which of the following is an uncountable noun?
   (A) Cattle   (B) Boy
   (C) Star   (D) Milk

6. Which of the following is a concrete noun?
   (A) Lies   (B) Forest
   (C) Bottle   (D) Sweet

7. Which of the following is a material noun?
   (A) Feathers   (B) Light
   (C) Air   (D) Deer

8. Which of the following is a countable noun?
   (A) Shadow   (B) Studio
   (C) Tea   (D) Red

9. Which of the following is a collective noun?
   (A) Team   (B) Rugby
   (C) Sugar   (D) Happiness

10. Which of the following is a proper noun?
    (A) Whale   (B) Velvet
    (C) Taiwan   (D) Perfume

II. Choose the correct option according to the instruction given in brackets.

11. Do you ever need to give request? (Which word is a count noun?)
    (A) Ever   (B) Give
    (C) Request   (D) You

12. Teacher asked students to use colour pencils during art period. (Which word is a compound noun?)
    (A) Colour pencil   (B) Students
    (C) Period   (D) Teacher

13. Australian government will bring tougher anti-terror laws. (Which word is a nominative noun?)
    (A) Bring   (B) Australian
    (C) Anti-terror   (D) Government

14. They like swimming. Whenever they have a leisure time. (Which word is a verbal noun?)
(A) Leisure   (B) Free
(C) Like   (D) Swimming

15. Solar energy can be an alternative source of power. (Which word is a predicative noun?)
(A) Solar
(B) Can be
(C) Alternative source of power
(D) Energy

16. Mice can nibble the food. (Which word is a plural possessive noun?)
(A) Can   (B) Mice
(C) Nibble   (D) The

17. Be careful, there is a hive of bees on tree. (Which word is a collective noun?)
(A) Tree   (B) There
(C) Hive of bees   (D) Careful

18. "O, you pass me my ball, buddy." (Which word is a naming noun?)
(A) My   (B) Pass
(C) Buddy   (D) You

19. Good friends are beauty of life. (Which word is a countable noun?)
(A) Friends   (B) Good
(C) Beauty   (D) Are

20. My grandmother is good at telling funny stories. (Which word is a plural noun?)
(A) Telling   (B) Stories
(C) Funny   (D) Goad

III. Directions (21-30): Determine the type of noun the italicized word and choose the correct option. Be careful, some of them are not nouns.

21. What type of noun is the word *Moon* as it is used in the following sentence?

Scientists believe that the Moon formed from an ancient planet called Theia that collided with the Earth billions of years ago.

(A) Singular noun   (B) Plural noun
(C) Possessive noun   (D) Not a noun

22. What type of noun is the word *Neil* as it is used in the following sentence?

Neil Armstrong is remembered for being the first person to walk on the Moon and for he memorable words that he spoke: "That's one small step for a man, one giant leap for mankind."

(A) Proper noun   (B) Plural noun
(C) Possessive noun   (D) Not a noun

23. What type of noun is the word *Halley's* as it is used in the following sentence?

At every 76th year or so, Earthlings have a chance to view Halley's Comet with the naked eye, and (assuming that you are an Earthling) your next chance will be in middle of the year 2061.

(A) Proper noun   (B) Plural noun
(C) Possessive noun   (D) Not a noun

24. What type of noun is the word *Pluto's* as it is used in the following sentence?

Pluto's status as a planet was called into question after numerous icy objects similar to Pluto were found orbiting the Sun.

(A) Singular noun   (B) Plural noun
(C) Possessive noun   (D) Not a noun

25. What type of noun is the word *galaxies* as it is used in the following sentence?

The Milky Way is the galaxy in which we live, but there are billions of galaxies in the known Universe.

(A) Singular noun   (B) Plural noun
(C) Possessive noun   (D) Not a noun

26. What type of noun is the word *crashes* as it is used in the following sentence?

A meteoroid becomes a meteorite when it crashes into the Earth.

(A) Singular noun   (B) Plural noun
(C) Possessive noun   (D) Not a noun

27. What type of noun is the word *Saturn's* as it is used in the following sentence?

Saturn's rings are made almost entirely

of ice, though they have traces of rocky material.

(A) Singular noun (B) Plural noun
(C) Possessive noun (D) Not a noun

28. What type of noun is the word *expanding* as it is used in the following sentence?

Edwin Hubble is best remembered for proving that the Universe is expanding.

(A) Singular noun (B) Plural noun
(C) Possessive noun (D) Not a noun

29. What type of noun is the word *night* as it is used in the following sentence?

The North Star is closely aligned with Earth's axis of rotation, so its position in the sky changes very little throughout the night.

(A) Singular noun (B) Plural noun
(C) Possessive noun (D) Not a noun

30. What type of noun is the word *effects* as it is used in the following sentence?

No one has ever seen a black hole with their own eyes, but scientists believe that they have witnessed their effects.

(A) Singular noun
(B) Plural noun
(C) Possessive noun
(D) Not a noun

HOTS (ACHIEVERS SECTION)

Fill in the blanks with the correct pronoun.

31. It took ____________ twenty minutes to get dressed.
   (A) I (B) me
   (C) us (D) none of these

32. She told _________ an interesting story.
   (A) I
   (B) me
   (C) us
   (D) none of these

33. I don't think we should wait for ________
   (A) he (B) him
   (C) us (D) none of these

34. You pay for your drinks and I will pay for ___________
   (A) mine (B) my
   (C) us (D) none of these

35. I am angry with both of ___________
   (A) they (B) them
   (C) me (D) none of these

ADJECTIVES

- ➤ Adjectives of Quality
- ➤ Adjectives of Quantity
- ➤ Adjectives of Numbers
- ➤ Other key types of Adjectives
- ➤ Comparison of Adjectives
- ➤ Usage of Adjectives

PRACTICE EXERCISE

Fill in the blanks with the correct option.

1. Generally, girls are _______ than boys.
   - (A) talkative
   - (B) more talkative
   - (C) most talkative
   - (D) none of these

2. Cricket is an _______ game.
   - (A) exciting
   - (B) more exciting
   - (C) most exciting
   - (D) none of these

3. Arpita is looking _______ in this dress.
   - (A) gorgeous
   - (B) gorgeouser
   - (C) gorgeousest
   - (D) none of these

4. She has a very _______ voice.
   - (A) sour
   - (B) bitter
   - (C) sweet
   - (D) none of these

5. Diamond is the _______ natural material.
   - (A) hard
   - (B) harder
   - (C) hardest
   - (D) none of these

6. This exercise is quite _______.
   - (A) simple
   - (B) more simple
   - (C) most simple
   - (D) none of these

7. Rohan is a _______ boy.
   - (A) trustworthy
   - (B) trustworthier
   - (C) trustworthiest
   - (D) none of these

8. The entire staff of the hotel we stayed at was very _______.
   - (A) friendly
   - (B) friendlier
   - (C) friendliest
   - (D) none of these

9. You are getting _______ all the time!
   - (A) good
   - (B) better
   - (C) best
   - (D) none of these

10. Your efforts to accomplish this project are _______!
    - (A) outstanding
    - (B) more outstanding
    - (C) most outstanding
    - (D) none of these

11. An elephant's brain is _______ a whale's brain.
    - (A) big than
    - (B) bigger than
    - (C) biggest
    - (D) more big than

12. Monkeys are ______ learners than elephants.
   (A) faster
   (B) very fast
   (C) more fast
   (D) more faster

13. I am ______ my brother.
   (A) taller than
   (B) more taller than
   (C) tallest
   (D) more taller than

14. Tom thinks that his car is ______ than my car.
   (A) expensiver
   (B) more expensiver
   (C) most expensive
   (D) more expensive

15. This examination is ______ than the other examination.
   (A) more easy
   (B) more difficult
   (C) more easier
   (D) most easy

16. David is ______ than Emily. Emily is arrogant.
   (A) more modest
   (B) modest
   (C) most modest
   (D) arrogant

17. My town is ______ this city.
   (A) more peaceful
   (B) peacefuller
   (C) more peaceful than
   (D) most peaceful

18. The test says that Mark is more ______ Becky.
   (A) taller
   (B) creative than

   (C) faster than
   (D) happier than

19. Some students are more ______ than others.
   (A) cleverer   (B) braver
   (C) slower   (D) successful

20. I was ill yesterday but I am ______ today.
   (A) bitter   (B) weller
   (C) better   (D) gooder

21. I don't have ______ much time for reading ______ I would like to.
   (A) as/as   (B) more/than
   (c) too/than   (d) so/than

22. English is today the third ______ native language worldwide after Chinese and Hindi, with some 380 million speakers.
   (A) the most spoken
   (B) the more spoken
   (C) much spoken
   (D) most spoken

23. My students' sleepless nights became ______ as the finals approached.
   (A) so frequently
   (B) more frequent
   (C) as frequent
   (d) much more frequent

24. It is often said that the hyena is an aggressive animal, but in fact it is not ______ many people believe.
   (A) more vicious   (B) so vicious that
   (C) as viciously as   (D) so vicious as

25. The roots of the old tree had spread out ______ thirty metres in all directions and had damaged nearby buildings.
   (A) as much as
   (B) so much
   (C) as many as
   (D) so many as

Read the passage given below and select options correctly replacing the underlined portions.

The many _______26_______ products of wetlands generate numerous _______27_______ benefits that are important for the livelihood of _______28_______ communities. Wetlands supply water for _______29_______ use, fisheries, forage resources, craft materials and medicinal plants. Wetlands are also treasured for their _______30_______ value. They are wonderful places to visit. Their pristine natural beauty make them a favorite haunt of tourists.

26.
(A) unique   (B) ubiquitous
(C) Diverse   (D) fashionable

27.
(A) neo-cultural   (B) antiquated
(C) socio-economic   (D) ultra-modern

28.
(A) local   (B) minor
(C) large   (D) popular

29.
(A) agricultural   (B) commercial
(C) Domestic   (D) agrarian

30.
(A) aesthetic   (B) commercial
(C) High   (D) low

Darken Your Choice with HB Pencil

1.	A B C D	7.	A B C D	13.	A B C D	19	A B C D	25.	A B C D
2.	A B C D	8.	A B C D	14.	A B C D	20.	A B C D	26.	A B C D
3.	A B C D	9.	A B C D	15.	A B C D	21.	A B C D	27.	A B C D
4.	A B C D	10.	A B C D	16.	A B C D	22.	A B C D	28.	A B C D
5.	A B C D	11.	A B C D	17.	A B C D	23.	A B C D	29.	A B C D
6.	A B C D	12.	A B C D	18.	A B C D	24.	A B C D	30.	A B C D

ARTICLES AND PREPOSITIONS

LEARNING OBJECTIVES

➤ Kinds of Articles
➤ Uses of Articles

➤ Preposition and its types
➤ Uses of Preposition

PRACTICE EXERCISE

I. Choose the correct option (article) to fill in the blanks.

1. Where's _______ knife I was just using?
   (A) no article needed
   (B) the
   (C) a
   (D) an

2. How much _______ snow do you get in winter?
   (A) a needed
   (B) no article
   (C) the
   (D) an

3. I had _______ fruit for lunch.
   (A) no article needed
   (B) the
   (C) a
   (D) an

4. I'm thinking about taking ___ holiday.
   (A) a
   (B) the
   (C) no article needed
   (D) an

5. Can you lend me _______ pen?
   (A) an
   (B) a
   (C) no article needed
   (D) the

6. ___ roses in your garden are beautiful.
   (A) the
   (B) an
   (C) no article needed
   (D) a

7. Make sure you drink plenty of _______ water.
   (A) no article needed
   (B) the
   (C) a
   (D) an

8. Let's eat out at _______ restaurant tonight. What type shall we go to?
   (A) no article needed
   (B) the
   (C) a
   (D) an

9. I should buy _______ new pair of shoes soon.
   (A) a
   (B) the
   (C) no article needed
   (D) an

II. Fill in the blanks with the correct article.

10. My father is ____ doctor and my mother is ____ artist.

11. I recommended _______ musician to Priya but she didn't like ______ artist at all.

12. There is ____ English and Hindi Thesaurus.

13. I met ______ editor and _______ cartoonist of _____ magazine.

14. I am ______ Indian by birth.

15. Eric is ____ star football player as well as ____ impressive captain.

16. My father is ________ honorable person.

17. I saw ______ monkey and ______ elephant at ____ zoo.

18. Varanasi is ________ holy place.

19. There's ______ peacock on _______ fence.

III. Fill in the blanks with A, An or (X) for 'no article'.

20. I have _______ two sisters and _______ brother. My brother has _______ son. That makes me _______ uncle.

21. Would you like _______ orange? Or would you prefer _______ banana? We also have _______ strawberries.

22. Does anyone have _______ cell phone? I need to make ______ emergency phone call.

23. John doesn't own _______ car. He rides _______ motorcycle to work.

24. Today, you ate _______ ice cream cone, _______ piece of pizza, _______ burrito and _______ donuts. That's not exactly _______ healthy diet.

25. Let's go see _______ movie. There's _______ adventure film that I have really been wanting to see.

26. Is there _______ Internet cafe around here? I need to send ______ important email.

27. Instead of making _______ traditional turkey for Thanksgiving dinner, she baked _______ enormous chicken.

28. It looks like it is going to be _______ rainy day. You should take _______ umbrella.

29. Phil and Debbie took _______ amazing vacation to Switzerland last year. They even climbed _______ mountain near Lucerne.

30. Because there was _______ huge rainstorm, the flight was delayed for more than _______ hour. The airport was full of _______ angry passengers.

HOTS (ACHIEVERS SECTION)

Fill in the blanks with the most suitable articles:

31. ________ ignorance is a bliss and ________ ignorance of Miranda was really astounding.
    (A) The, the
    (B) No article, the
    (C) No article, no article
    (D) An, the

32. We were admiring ______ beauty of Cleopatra but my friend said, "______ beauty is skin deep."
    (A) the, no article
    (B) the, the
    (C) no article, no article
    (D) a, the

33. In scientific experiments ______ accuracy is essential and John could not judge ______ accuracy of the calculations.
    (A) an, the
    (B) no article, an
    (C) no article, the
    (D) no article, no article

34. Water is necessary for ______ life but ______ life of these insects does not depend on water.
   (A) no article, no article
   (B) no article the
   (C) the, the
   (D) a, the

35. ______ Amazon is ______ longest river in the world.
   (A) The, the
   (B) No article, the
   (C) No article, no article
   (D) The, no article

1.	Ⓐ Ⓑ Ⓒ Ⓓ	8.	Ⓐ Ⓑ Ⓒ Ⓓ	15.	Ⓐ Ⓑ Ⓒ Ⓓ	22.	Ⓐ Ⓑ Ⓒ Ⓓ	29.	Ⓐ Ⓑ Ⓒ Ⓓ
2.	Ⓐ Ⓑ Ⓒ Ⓓ	9.	Ⓐ Ⓑ Ⓒ Ⓓ	16.	Ⓐ Ⓑ Ⓒ Ⓓ	23.	Ⓐ Ⓑ Ⓒ Ⓓ	30.	Ⓐ Ⓑ Ⓒ Ⓓ
3.	Ⓐ Ⓑ Ⓒ Ⓓ	10.	Ⓐ Ⓑ Ⓒ Ⓓ	17.	Ⓐ Ⓑ Ⓒ Ⓓ	24.	Ⓐ Ⓑ Ⓒ Ⓓ	31.	Ⓐ Ⓑ Ⓒ Ⓓ
4.	Ⓐ Ⓑ Ⓒ Ⓓ	11.	Ⓐ Ⓑ Ⓒ Ⓓ	18.	Ⓐ Ⓑ Ⓒ Ⓓ	25.	Ⓐ Ⓑ Ⓒ Ⓓ	32.	Ⓐ Ⓑ Ⓒ Ⓓ
5.	Ⓐ Ⓑ Ⓒ Ⓓ	12.	Ⓐ Ⓑ Ⓒ Ⓓ	19.	Ⓐ Ⓑ Ⓒ Ⓓ	26.	Ⓐ Ⓑ Ⓒ Ⓓ	33.	Ⓐ Ⓑ Ⓒ Ⓓ
6.	Ⓐ Ⓑ Ⓒ Ⓓ	13.	Ⓐ Ⓑ Ⓒ Ⓓ	20.	Ⓐ Ⓑ Ⓒ Ⓓ	27.	Ⓐ Ⓑ Ⓒ Ⓓ	34.	Ⓐ Ⓑ Ⓒ Ⓓ
7.	Ⓐ Ⓑ Ⓒ Ⓓ	14.	Ⓐ Ⓑ Ⓒ Ⓓ	21.	Ⓐ Ⓑ Ⓒ Ⓓ	28.	Ⓐ Ⓑ Ⓒ Ⓓ	35.	Ⓐ Ⓑ Ⓒ Ⓓ

CONJUNCTION AND DETERMINERS

LEARNING OBJECTIVES

➤ Conjunctions
➤ Determiners

PRACTICE EXERCISE

1. Fill in the blanks with the most appropriate conjunctions:

   Heera _____ his parents are well-educated.

   (A) and   (B) but

   (C) as well as   (D) nor

2. Fill in the blanks with the most appropriate conjunctions:

   The culprit was _____ fined and punished.

   (A) also   (B) and

   (C) but   (D) both

3. Fill in the blanks with the most appropriate conjunctions:

   _____ the boys concentrate, they can't learn Kung Fu.

   (A) Until   (B) Till

   (C) Unless   (D) If

4. Fill in the blanks with the most appropriate conjunctions:

   _____ my uncle is old, he thinks like a child.

   (A) But   (B) That

   (C) Although   (D) As

5. Fill in the blanks with the most appropriate conjunctions:

   Rocky is wasting his money _____ his parents are starving.

   (A) than   (B) then

   (C) while   (D) since

6. Fill in the blanks with the most appropriate conjunctions:

   Krish was absent from the office _____ he was dismissed.

   (A) since   (B) for

   (C) however   (D) therefore

7. Fill in the blanks with the most appropriate conjunctions:

   The baby is crying _____ it is hungry.

   (A) because   (B) yet

   (C) though   (D) or

8. Fill in the blanks with the most appropriate conjunctions:

   _____ difficult the problem is, one must not lose hope.

   (A) Whether   (B) However

   (C) As far as   (D) Though

9. Fill in the blanks with the most appropriate conjunctions:

   Do you know _____ the magician performed the trick?

   (A) how   (B) however

   (C) whenever   (D) that

OLYMPIAD WORKBOOK (IEO) CLASS – 9

10. Fill in the blanks with the most appropriate conjunctions:

_____ we are working, we are happy and healthy.

(A) As far as
(B) As long as
(C) In case
(D) Nevertheless

11. Fill in the blanks with the most suitable determiners:

The two boys walked in, _____ one carrying flowers.

(A) each
(B) every
(C) with
(D) both A and B

12. Fill in the blanks with the most suitable determiners:

The minister has virtually presided over _____ meeting for the last ten years.

(A) each
(B) every
(C) all
(D) both A and B

13. Fill in the blanks with the most suitable determiners:

Jane didn't buy any oranges but I purchased

(A) any
(B) some
(C) few
(D) little

14. Fill in the blanks with the most suitable determiners:

Who did you meet? I met _____.

(A) none
(B) anybody
(C) no one
(D) some

15. Fill in the blanks with the most suitable determiners:

"How much money have you got?" I asked Jack. He replied, "_______."

(A) None
(B) Any
(C) No one
(D) Few

16. Fill in the blanks with the most suitable determiners:

Leena said _____, but I couldn't understand what she said.

(A) something
(B) anything
(C) nothing
(D) someone

17. Fill in the blanks with the most suitable determiners:

Mary speaks French well because she lived in France for _____ years.

(A) much
(B) a few
(C) few
(D) any

18. Fill in the blanks with the most suitable determiners:

Saurabh is a very unsocial person so _____ people know him well.

(A) many
(B) a few
(C) few
(D) no one

19. Fill in the blanks with the most suitable determiners:

Vikky doesn't work hard, so there is _____ hope for his success.

(A) little
(B) a little
(C) the little
(D) some

20. Fill in the blanks with the most suitable determiners:

There isn't _____ ink in this ink-pot.

(A) some
(B) little
(C) any
(D) many

Read the passages below and select respective options that can correctly replace the underlined portions.

In the past, tigers were considered as pests. _______21_______ a smaller area to hunt, when man had taken up more of the land to build upon, the tigers found less areas for themselves to hunt. They _______22_______ turned to farms to get their food. Farmers' livestock were attacked by these tigers. People were then encouraged to kill the animals with the promise of rewards. _______23_______ the threat of tigers on livestock was over, man continued to hunt tigers, now for recreation. Poachers knowing that the skin of tigers is much sought after _______24_______, hunt tigers _______25_______ their body parts. Bones and other organs are both used as ingredients in traditional Chinese medicine.

21.
(A) For (B) When
(C) With (D) Yet

22.
(A) yet (B) consequently
(C) Thus (D) therefore

23.
(A) Even if (B) Since
(C) Despite (D) Even after

24.
(A) and (B) too
(C) But (D) since

25.
(A) not only (B) both
(C) For (D) also

Darken Your Choice with HB Pencil

	A B C D		A B C D		A B C D		A B C D		A B C D
1.	Ⓐ Ⓑ Ⓒ Ⓓ	6.	Ⓐ Ⓑ Ⓒ Ⓓ	11.	Ⓐ Ⓑ Ⓒ Ⓓ	16	Ⓐ Ⓑ Ⓒ Ⓓ	21.	Ⓐ Ⓑ Ⓒ Ⓓ
2.	Ⓐ Ⓑ Ⓒ Ⓓ	7.	Ⓐ Ⓑ Ⓒ Ⓓ	12.	Ⓐ Ⓑ Ⓒ Ⓓ	17.	Ⓐ Ⓑ Ⓒ Ⓓ	22.	Ⓐ Ⓑ Ⓒ Ⓓ
3.	Ⓐ Ⓑ Ⓒ Ⓓ	8.	Ⓐ Ⓑ Ⓒ Ⓓ	13.	Ⓐ Ⓑ Ⓒ Ⓓ	18.	Ⓐ Ⓑ Ⓒ Ⓓ	23.	Ⓐ Ⓑ Ⓒ Ⓓ
4.	Ⓐ Ⓑ Ⓒ Ⓓ	9.	Ⓐ Ⓑ Ⓒ Ⓓ	14.	Ⓐ Ⓑ Ⓒ Ⓓ	19.	Ⓐ Ⓑ Ⓒ Ⓓ	24.	Ⓐ Ⓑ Ⓒ Ⓓ
5.	Ⓐ Ⓑ Ⓒ Ⓓ	10.	Ⓐ Ⓑ Ⓒ Ⓓ	15.	Ⓐ Ⓑ Ⓒ Ⓓ	20.	Ⓐ Ⓑ Ⓒ Ⓓ	25.	Ⓐ Ⓑ Ⓒ Ⓓ

SENTENCE SEQUENCING

LEARNING OBJECTIVES

➤ Sequence sentencing
➤ Alternative words/phrase

PRACTICE EXERCISE

1. Fill in the blanks with the appropriate alternatives:
    The cat does not like swimming much, _____?
    (A) did it   (B) does it
    (C) was it   (D) were it

2. Fill in the blanks with the appropriate alternatives:
    We can leave our bags in the class, _____?
    (A) can we   (B) can't we
    (C) could we   (D) couldn't we

3. Fill in the blanks with the appropriate alternatives:
    The food at the party was delicious, _____?
    (A) wasn't it   (B) weren't it
    (C) was it   (D) were it

4. Fill in the blanks with the appropriate alternatives:
    I am not too old, _____?
    (A) am I   (B) are I
    (C) were I   (D) was I

5. Fill in the blanks with the appropriate alternatives:
    The papers weren't very tough, _____?
    (A) are they   (B) were they
    (C) isn't it   (D) is it

6. Fill in the blanks with the appropriate alternatives:
    You aren't eighteen yet, _____?
    (A) are you   (B) is you
    (C) were you (D) will you

7. Fill in the blanks with the appropriate alternatives:
    There are a lot of books in the library, _____?
    (A) are there   (B) aren't there
    (C) is there   (D) isn't there

8. Fill in the blanks with the appropriate alternatives:
    There was no one at home, _____?
    (A) is there   (B) were there
    (C) isn't there (D) was there

9. Fill in the blanks with the appropriate alternatives:
    The picnic was good fun, _____?
    (A) was it   (B) wasn't it
    (C) were it   (D) weren't it

10. Fill in the blanks with the appropriate alternatives:
    Aditya is growing tall, _____?
    (A) is he   (B) isn't he
    (C) will he   (D) won't he

11. Fill in the blanks with the appropriate alternatives:

We mustn't be late, _____?

(A) mustn't we   (B) could we

(C) couldn't we   (D) must we

12. Fill in the blanks with the appropriate alternatives:

You could help me carry these water bottles to the third floor, _____?

(A) couldn't you   (B) will you

(C) could you   (D) would you

13. Reorder the given phrases to make meaningful sentences out of them:

P. a

Q. empty house

R. boy walked

S. into an

(A) P-Q-R-S   (B) P-R-S-Q

(C) P-S-R-Q   (D) S-R-Q-P

14. Reorder the given phrases to make meaningful sentences out of them:

P. food

Q. the dining table

R. there was

S. lying on

(A) P-Q-R-S   (B) S-R-Q-P

(C) R-P-S-Q   (D) Q-S-P-R

15. Reorder the given phrases to make meaningful sentences out of them:

P. her eyesight became

Q. using spectacles

R. with growing age,

S. started

T. weak so she

(A) P-Q-R-S-T   (B) P-S-T-Q-R

(C) R-P-T-S-Q   (D) S-Q-P-R-T

16. Reorder the given phrases to make meaningful sentences out of them:

P. grown quite a bit

Q. over the

R. Rita has

S. last fifteen years

(A) P-Q-R-S   (B) Q-S-R-P

(C) P-S-Q-R   (D) S-R-Q-P

17. Reorder the given phrases to make meaningful sentences out of them:

P. scooter for

Q. also got a

R. herself now

S. she has

(A) P-Q-R-S   (B) S-R-Q-P

(C) S-Q-R-P   (D) S-Q-P-R

18. Reorder the given phrases to make meaningful sentences out of them:

P. already signed the contract

Q. to change his mind

R. it's too late

S. and the deal is complete

T. as he has

(A) R-P-S-T-Q   (B) R-Q-T-P-S

(C) T-Q-P-S-R   (D) P-Q-R-S-T

19. Reorder the given phrases to make meaningful sentences out of them:

P. people

Q. stay at home

R. public

S. who act in

T. should

(A) P-S-R-T-Q   (B) P-S-Q-R-T

(C) P-Q-R-S-T   (D) P-T-Q-R-S

20. Reorder the given phrases to make meaningful sentences out of them:

P. time

Q. is nature's way

R. of preventing everything from happening

S. all at once

(A) P-S-Q-R   (B) P-Q-S-R

(C) P-Q-R-S   (D) R-P-Q-S

21. Reorder the given phrases to make meaningful sentences out of them:
   P. all buying
   Q. that company
   R. more shares in
   S. we're
   (A) P-S-R-Q
   (B) S-P-R-Q
   (C) S-R-Q-P
   (D) P-Q-R-S

22. Reorder the given phrases to make meaningful sentences out of them:
   P. as expected, but
   Q. our manufacturing division
   R. all in all
   S. we had a good year
   T. didn't do as well
   (A) P-Q-R-S-T
   (B) P-Q-T-R-S
   (C) T-S-R-Q-P
   (D) Q-T-P-R-S

23. Reorder the given phrases to make meaningful sentences out of them:
   P. McDonald's restaurants
   Q. in India
   R. now
   S. there are
   T. all over
   (A) R-S-P-T-Q
   (B) R-T-Q-P-S
   (C) P-Q-R-S-T
   (D) T-S-R-Q-P

24. Reorder the given phrases to make meaningful sentences out of them:
   P. he is going to
   Q. but he is all
   R. Ajay says that
   S. talk and no action
   T. lose weight
   (A) P-T-S-Q-R
   (B) R-P-T-Q-S
   (C) T-R-P-S-Q
   (D) P-Q-R-S-T

25. Reorder the given phrases to make meaningful sentences out of them:
   P. as many as
   Q. will consist of
   R. Fifteen people
   S. the team
   (A) S-Q-R-P
   (B) S-R-P-Q
   (C) P-S-Q-R
   (D) S-Q-P-R

1.	(A) (B) (C) (D)	6.	(A) (B) (C) (D)	11.	(A) (B) (C) (D)	16.	(A) (B) (C) (D)	21.	(A) (B) (C) (D)
2.	(A) (B) (C) (D)	7.	(A) (B) (C) (D)	12.	(A) (B) (C) (D)	17.	(A) (B) (C) (D)	22.	(A) (B) (C) (D)
3.	(A) (B) (C) (D)	8.	(A) (B) (C) (D)	13.	(A) (B) (C) (D)	18.	(A) (B) (C) (D)	23.	(A) (B) (C) (D)
4.	(A) (B) (C) (D)	9.	(A) (B) (C) (D)	14.	(A) (B) (C) (D)	19.	(A) (B) (C) (D)	24.	(A) (B) (C) (D)
5.	(A) (B) (C) (D)	10.	(A) (B) (C) (D)	15.	(A) (B) (C) (D)	20.	(A) (B) (C) (D)	25.	(A) (B) (C) (D)

Darken Your Choice with HB Pencil

TENSES AND CONDITIONALS

LEARNING OBJECTIVES

➤ Basic concepts of Tenses
➤ Different types of Tenses
➤ Concept of Conditional Sentences

PRACTICE EXERCISE

I. Fill in blanks with the correct form of verb.

1. Although the police __________ every precaution, the robber managed to escape.
   (A) take   (B) takes
   (C) has taken   (D) had taken

2. The boys ______ television every night unless they have homework.
   (A) watch   (B) watches
   (C) watched   (D) watching

3. Maria ______ an appointment to see the doctor. It is at 10.00 am. tomorrow.
   (A) make   (B) makes
   (C) made   (D) has made

4. They ______ when they are ready.
   (A) come   (B) came
   (C) will come   (D) have come

5. Reena ______ watching horror films although she has nightmares afterwards.
   (A) like   (B) likes
   (C) liked   (D) will like

6. It ______ every afternoon for the past week. The weather forecast predicts rain for next week too.
   (A) is raining
   (B) was raining

   (C) has been raining
   (D) had been raining

7. I ______ the door before I realized that the keys were inside the house.
   (A) lock   (B) locked
   (C) has locked   (D) had locked

8. When Sally ______ her first pay, she bought presents for her parents.
   (A) receive   (B) received
   (C) has received   (D) had received

9. It's lovely to wake up in the morning and ______ birds singing.
   (A) hear   (B) hears
   (C) heard   (D) hearing

10. Shivam ______ $80.00 for that bag.
    (A) pay   (B) paid
    (C) pays   (D) paying

11. When I went back to my hometown three years ago, I found that a lot of changes ______.
    (A) are taken place
    (B) were taken place
    (C) have taken place
    (D) had taken place

12. Look ! A hamster ______ by a cat.
    (A) is chased
    (B) is being chased

(C) was being chased
(D) has been chased

13. I'm sorry the house is not available any longer. It ______ to a timber tycoon.
    (A) is sold
    (B) was being sold
    (C) has been sold
    (D) will be sold

14. Ai Ling ______ to Manhattan in 1997.
    (A) is transferred
    (B) was transferred
    (C) has been transferred
    (D) should be transferred

15. Passengers ______ to smoke in the train.
    (A) are not allowed
    (B) was not allowed
    (C) had not allowed
    (D) will not allow

16. Firemen who battled the fire reported that it______ under control after forty minutes.
    (A) is brought
    (B) was brought
    (C) can be brought
    (D) has been brought

17. The students ______ to leave the building immediately.
    (A) ordered
    (B) will order
    (C) have ordered
    (D) have been ordered

18. In future, famous singers ______ to perform at charity concerts.
    (A) are invited
    (B) were invited
    (C) has been invited
    (D) will be invited

19. The roof may have been leaking for the past few weeks but you do not have to worry about it any longer. It ______ now.
    (A) was repaired

(B) is repairing
(C) has repaired
(D) is being repaired

20. The price ______, but I doubt whether it will remain so.
    (A) went down   (B) will go down
    (C) has gone down   (D) was going down

21. My mother ______ biscuits from the shop once a week.
    (A) is buying
    (B) has bought
    (C) buys
    (D) will have bought

22. The groom, together with his parents, ______ the guests.
    (A) is greeting   (B) have greeted
    (C) are greeting   (D) were greeting

23. None of the new equipment ______ yet.
    (A) has arrived   (B) have arrived
    (C) were arriving   (D) are arriving

24. ______ she ______ a lot of friends at the party?
    (A) Does, makes   (B) Did, make
    (C) Did, made   (D) Do, make

25. Nobody ______ the telephone an hour ago.
    (A) is using   (B) were using
    (C) was using   (D) has used

26. If I ______ some money I would not have to borrow now.
    (A) am saving   (B) have saved
    (C) saved   (D) had saved

27. A river ______ downstream.
    (A) flows   (B) will flow
    (C) is flowing   (D) was flowing

28. She ______ a maid by next year.
    (A) employs
    (B) employed
    (C) has employed
    (D) will have employed

29. He _______ never _______ since he nearly
    _______ .
    (A) has, swum, drowned
    (B) had, swum, was drowning
    (C) was, swimming, drowned
    (D) did, swum, had drowned

30. We _______ jungle-trekking.
    (A) are disliking
    (B) have disliked
    (C) dislike
    (D) were disliking

HOTS (ACHIEVERS SECTION)

Fill in the blanks with the correct form of verb using simple present or present continuous tense.

31. Look! Sarah (go) _______ to the movies.

32. On her right hand, Sarah (carry) _________ her handbag.

33. The handbag (be) ___very beautiful.

34. Sarah usually (put) _____on black shoes but now she (wear) ________white trainers.

35. She (take) ________an umbrella because it (rain) _______.

1.	A B C D	8.	A B C D	15.	A B C D	22	A B C D	29.	A B C D
2.	A B C D	9.	A B C D	16.	A B C D	23.	A B C D	30.	A B C D
3.	A B C D	10.	A B C D	17.	A B C D	24.	A B C D	31.	A B C D
4.	A B C D	11.	A B C D	18.	A B C D	25.	A B C D	32.	A B C D
5.	A B C D	12.	A B C D	19.	A B C D	26.	A B C D	33.	A B C D
6.	A B C D	13.	A B C D	20.	A B C D	27.	A B C D	34.	A B C D
7.	A B C D	14.	A B C D	21.	A B C D	28.	A B C D	35.	A B C D

VOICE AND NARRATION 

LEARNING OBJECTIVES

➤ Voice and its two different types – Active and Passive
➤ Reporter Speech – Direct and Indirect

PRACTICE EXERCISE

I. Fill in the blanks with suitable active and passive verb forms.

1. This house ____________ in 1970 by my grandfather.
   (A) built
   (B) was built
   (C) was build
   (D) has built

2. The robbers ___________ by the police.
   (A) have arrested
   (B) have been arrested
   (C) was arrested
   (D) had arrested

3. We ___________ for the examination.
   (A) have preparing
   (B) are preparing
   (C) had preparing
   (D) have been prepared

4. It ___________ since yesterday.
   (A) is raining
   (B) has been raining
   (C) have been raining
   (D) was raining

5. I ___________ for five hours.
   (A) have been working
   (B) has been working
   (C) was working
   (D) am working

6. The students ___________ to submit their reports by the end of this week.
   (A) have asked
   (B) are asked
   (C) has asked
   (D) are asking

7. She ___________ for a while.
   (A) are ailing
   (B) is ailing
   (C) has been ailing
   (D) have been ailing

8. The teacher ___________ the student for lying.
   (A) has been punished
   (B) punished
   (C) is punished
   (D) was punished

9. I _______ to become a successful writer.
   (A) have always wanted
   (B) am always wanted
   (C) was always wanted
   (D) am always wanting

10. The inmates of the juvenile home _________ well by their caretakers.
   (A) were not being treated
   (B) were not treating
   (C) have not being treated
   (D) was not being treated

11. As the patient could not walk he _________ home in a wheel chair.
   (A) has carried
   (B) has been carried
   (C) was carried
   (D) was carrying

12. The injured _________ to the hospital in an ambulance.
   (A) were taking
   (B) was taking
   (C) were taken
   (D) have taken

II. Choose the option which best expresses the given sentence in Passive/Active voice.

13. You can play with these kittens quite safely.
   (A) These kittens can played with quite safely.
   (B) These kittens can play with you quite safely.
   (C) These kittens can be played with you quite safely.
   (D) These kittens can be played with quite safely.

14. A child could not have done this mischief.
   (A) This mischief could not be done by a child.
   (B) This mischief could not been done by a child.
   (C) This mischief could not have been done by a child.
   (D) This mischief a child could not have been done.

15. James Watt discovered the energy of steam.
   (A) The energy of steam discovered James Watt.
   (B) The energy of steam was discovered by James Watt.
   (C) James Watt was discovered by the energy of steam.
   (D) James Watt had discovered energy by the steam.

16. She makes cakes every Sunday.
   (A) Every Sunday cakes made by her.
   (B) Cakes are made by her every Sunday.
   (C) Cakes make her every Sunday.
   (D) Cakes were made by her every Sunday.

17. She spoke to the official on duty.
   (A) The official on duty was spoken to by her.
   (B) The official was spoken to by her on duty.
   (C) She was spoken to by the official on duty.
   (D) She was the official to be spoken to on duty.

18. The doctor advised the patient not to eat rice.
   (A) The patient was advised by the doctor not to eat rice.
   (B) The patient was advised by the doctor that he should not eat rice.
   (C) The patient was being advised by the doctor that he should not rice by the doctor.
   (D) The patient has been advised not to eat rice by the doctor.

19. I cannot accept your offer.
   (A) Your offer cannot be accepted by me.
   (B) I cannot be accepted by your offer.

(C) The offer cannot be accepted by me.

(D) Your offer cannot be accepted.

20. You should open the wine about three hours before you use it.

    (A) Wine should be opened about three hours before use.

    (B) Wine should be opened by you three hours before use.

    (C) Wine should be opened about three hours before you use it.

    (D) Wine should be opened about three hours before it is used.

21. They will inform the police.

    (A) The police will be informed by them.

    (B) The police will inform them.

    (C) The police are informed by them.

    (D) Informed will be the police by them.

22. Why do you tell a lie?

    (A) Why a lie told by you?

    (B) Why is a lie be told by you?

    (C) Why is a lie told by you?

    (D) Why is a lite being told you?

23. You will praise her very much.

    (A) She will praised very much by you.

    (B) She will be praised very much by you.

    (C) She will being praised very much by you.

    (D) She will been praised very much by you.

24. I take exercise daily.

    (A) Exercise are taken daily by me.

    (B) Exercise is taken daily by me.

    (C) Exercise is being taken daily by me.

    (D) Exercise is been taken daily by me.

25. She will invite me.

    (A) I shall be invited by her.

    (B) I will invited by her.

    (C) I shall being invited by her.

    (D) I will been invited by her.

26. Did you visit a zoo?

    (A) Was a zoo being visited by you?

    (B) Was a zoo be visited by you?

    (C) Was a zoo been visited by you?

    (D) Was a zoo visited by you?

27. Our task had been completed before sunset.

    (A) We completed our task before sunset.

    (B) We have completed our task before sunset.

    (C) We complete our task before sunset.

    (D) We had completed our task before sunset.

28. The boy laughed at the beggar.

    (A) The beggar was laughed by the boy.

    (B) The beggar was being laughed by the boy.

    (C) The beggar was being laughed at by the boy.

    (D) The beggar was laughed at by the boy.

29. The boys were playing Cricket.

    (A) Cricket had been played by the boys.

    (B) Cricket has been played by the boys.

    (C) Cricket was played by the boys.

    (D) Cricket was being played by the boys.

30. They drew a circle in the morning.

    (A) A circle was being drawn by them in the morning.

    (B) A circle was drawn by them in the morning.

    (C) In the morning a circle have been drawn by them.

    (D) A circle has been drawing since morning.

Find out the sentences that are written incorrectly in the passive voice.

31. I was eaten an ice cream.

32. The song was sung by a singer.

33. I was deceived by the TV program.

34. The concert was finished at 12 p.m.

35. He was written a novel.

—Darken Your Choice with HB Pencil—

1.	Ⓐ Ⓑ Ⓒ Ⓓ	8.	Ⓐ Ⓑ Ⓒ Ⓓ	15.	Ⓐ Ⓑ Ⓒ Ⓓ	22	Ⓐ Ⓑ Ⓒ Ⓓ	29.	Ⓐ Ⓑ Ⓒ Ⓓ
2.	Ⓐ Ⓑ Ⓒ Ⓓ	9.	Ⓐ Ⓑ Ⓒ Ⓓ	16.	Ⓐ Ⓑ Ⓒ Ⓓ	23.	Ⓐ Ⓑ Ⓒ Ⓓ	30.	Ⓐ Ⓑ Ⓒ Ⓓ
3.	Ⓐ Ⓑ Ⓒ Ⓓ	10.	Ⓐ Ⓑ Ⓒ Ⓓ	17.	Ⓐ Ⓑ Ⓒ Ⓓ	24.	Ⓐ Ⓑ Ⓒ Ⓓ	31.	Ⓐ Ⓑ Ⓒ Ⓓ
4.	Ⓐ Ⓑ Ⓒ Ⓓ	11.	Ⓐ Ⓑ Ⓒ Ⓓ	18.	Ⓐ Ⓑ Ⓒ Ⓓ	25.	Ⓐ Ⓑ Ⓒ Ⓓ	32.	Ⓐ Ⓑ Ⓒ Ⓓ
5.	Ⓐ Ⓑ Ⓒ Ⓓ	12.	Ⓐ Ⓑ Ⓒ Ⓓ	19.	Ⓐ Ⓑ Ⓒ Ⓓ	26.	Ⓐ Ⓑ Ⓒ Ⓓ	33.	Ⓐ Ⓑ Ⓒ Ⓓ
6.	Ⓐ Ⓑ Ⓒ Ⓓ	13.	Ⓐ Ⓑ Ⓒ Ⓓ	20.	Ⓐ Ⓑ Ⓒ Ⓓ	27.	Ⓐ Ⓑ Ⓒ Ⓓ	34.	Ⓐ Ⓑ Ⓒ Ⓓ
7.	Ⓐ Ⓑ Ⓒ Ⓓ	14.	Ⓐ Ⓑ Ⓒ Ⓓ	21.	Ⓐ Ⓑ Ⓒ Ⓓ	28.	Ⓐ Ⓑ Ⓒ Ⓓ	35.	Ⓐ Ⓑ Ⓒ Ⓓ

LEARNING OBJECTIVES

➤ Reading Comprehension

PRACTICE EXERCISE

I. CLASSIFIED

1. What is for sale?
   (A) A house   (B) pool
   (C) flat   (D) car

2. How far is Vasant Marg from the metro station?
   (A) three minutes   (B) three seconds
   (C) five minutes   (D) five seconds

3. Who are the brokers?
   (A) Estate officers
   (B) Their job is to find homes for people and vice versa
   (C) They are the middlemen for such deals
   (D) They tend to break into houses.

4. What is non-negotiable?
   (A) The space   (B) The price
   (C) The terrace   (D) The rent

5. What are the added benefits?
   (A) Terrace & garden
   (B) Garden and lift
   (C) Lift and terrace
   (D) Lift and pool

II. DICTIONARY

6. Where is this sort of text taken from?

7. What does the [*hay-loh*] portion of the text mean?

8. What sorts of differences are there between the definitions?

9. What is another name for halo?

III. HANDWRITING IN SCHOOL

Question:

10. Why is writing not given much importance today?

11. Why was the author taken aback when his daughter came home with her homework handwritten in cursive?

12. Why was cursive writing introduced?

13. How is taking notes better than typing?

14. What causes the 'bad habit' to be established?

15. What does the resurgence of fountain pen sales show?

16. Although children are taught to write at an early age, they do not have legible handwriting when they grow up as ______.

17. Learning your QWERTY means ______.

IV. ANN DAVISON

Question:

18. Give the meaning of the following words as used in the passage. One word answers or short phrases will be accepted.

    (A) morale   (B) consoled

    (C) deficiency

19. Answer the following questions briefly in your own words.

    (A) What was Ann Davison discovering about the learning of other long-distance sailors?

    (B) Why do you think the author says, "the sound was good for her morale"?

    (C) What did Ann Davison do when squall struck and she could not sail any more?

    (D) Why did Ann Davison decide to head for Barbados although she had originally planned for Antigua?

    (E) What exhausted her even more?

20. Give a character sketch of Ann Davison in your own words. Do not exceed 50 words.

Darken Your Choice with HB Pencil

1.	Ⓐ Ⓑ Ⓒ Ⓓ	5.	Ⓐ Ⓑ Ⓒ Ⓓ	9.	Ⓐ Ⓑ Ⓒ Ⓓ	13	Ⓐ Ⓑ Ⓒ Ⓓ	17.	Ⓐ Ⓑ Ⓒ Ⓓ
2.	Ⓐ Ⓑ Ⓒ Ⓓ	6.	Ⓐ Ⓑ Ⓒ Ⓓ	10.	Ⓐ Ⓑ Ⓒ Ⓓ	14.	Ⓐ Ⓑ Ⓒ Ⓓ	18.	Ⓐ Ⓑ Ⓒ Ⓓ
3.	Ⓐ Ⓑ Ⓒ Ⓓ	7.	Ⓐ Ⓑ Ⓒ Ⓓ	11.	Ⓐ Ⓑ Ⓒ Ⓓ	15.	Ⓐ Ⓑ Ⓒ Ⓓ	19.	Ⓐ Ⓑ Ⓒ Ⓓ
4.	Ⓐ Ⓑ Ⓒ Ⓓ	8.	Ⓐ Ⓑ Ⓒ Ⓓ	12.	Ⓐ Ⓑ Ⓒ Ⓓ	16.	Ⓐ Ⓑ Ⓒ Ⓓ	20.	Ⓐ Ⓑ Ⓒ Ⓓ

SPOKEN AND WRITTEN EXPRESSIONS; PUNCTUATION

LEARNING OBJECTIVES

➤ Basic concept of Punctuation
➤ Types of Punctuation
➤ Common Punctuation marks

PRACTICE EXERCISE

I. **Choose the best reply/option to the given statement:**

Example: Rita: Good morning! How are you feeling today?

Akhil:______________________

(A) Cool, thanks

(B) I'm doing okay so far. You?

(C) Fine, thank you! What about you?

The correct choice is, choice c, as it is polite and expresses thought for the person being spoken to.

1. Tourist: Excuse me, I'm a bit lost. Could you point me in the right direction?

   Annie:__________________

   (A) Yes, of course. Where would you like to go?

   (B) No, I'm busy.

   (C) Ya, sure.

2. Ankita: The weather is so pleasant today!

   Bhavya:__________________

   (A) So?

   (B) It is, isn't it?

   (C) I don't really care.

3. Aman: My phone isn't working properly.

   Store Attendant: ______________

   (A) I'm on a break.

   (B) Good afternoon! How may I help?

   (C) Wait for a while. I'm a bit busy now.

4. Carol: Thank you for passing the newspaper.

   Christine: ______________

   (A) Whatever.

   (B) Sure!

   (C) It's ok.

5. Anita: Why are you so late?

   Nima: ______________

   (A) Stop getting so angry over such a small issue.

   (B) I'm sorry, I got caught in heavy traffic.

   (C) I woke up late.

6. Shubham: I'm in so much trouble at home.

   Palak:__________________

   (A) Serves you right.

   (B) Doesn't matter. All of us are

   (C) Don't worry, it'll be fine

7. Sweta: Could you please help me move the boxes somewhere?

Shruti: ______________

(A) Yes, of course!

(B) No, it's too heavy for me, let me find someone who can.

(C) I don't feel like it. Sorry.

8. Aakash: I've cut my hand.

Raj:_________

(A) That's because you're so careless.

(B) Wait, let me find a band aid.

(C) Don't worry. It's barely a nick.

9. Rhea: I forgot my pen. May I borrow yours?

Sanchit: ____________

(A) Yes, here, I have an extra.

(B) No

(C) Sorry, I'm using it.

10. Aditya: That concert was so much funny!

Anshul:____________

(A) I didn't want to come.

(B) I don't care

(C) Surely it was funny!

II. Choose the correct option to answer each of the following questions.
How would you:

11. Talk to someone who's come to your country for the first time and isn't fluent with the language?

(A) Slowly and politely, being empathetic.

(B) Talking fast and forcing your opinion on the individual.

(C) Saying that you don't have the time.

(D) None of these

12. Give help a lost stranger?

(A) Pretend you can't hear her.

(B) Give incorrect directions because you aren't sure yourself.

(C) Help in any way possible.

(D) None of these

13. Address a complaint.

(A) Ignore it.

(B) Make excuses.

(C) Apologise and promise to correct the mistake.

(D) None of these

14. Give suggestions to a friend about clothes and colours that suit her/him.

(A) Tell them that they are colour blind and have no taste.

(B) Suggest new styles and colours which suit them better.

(C) Tell them that look okay.

15. Decline an invitation to a party.

(A) Say that you don't feel like coming.

(B) Lie about being ill and go somewhere else.

(C) Thank the host for invitation, and politely decline.

(D) None of these

III. Fill in the blanks with the correct conjunction.

16. You can come to the meeting ______ you don't say anything.

(A) so that

(B) as long as

(C) while

(d) as if

17. I'm not leaving ______ I get an apology from you.

(A) so that

(B) as long as

(C) until

(D) as if

18. I came here ______ you could give me an explanation.

(A) so that

(B) as long as

(C) while

(D) until

19. Rima is very tall _______ Mira is very short.
   (A) as if
   (B) as long as
   (C) while
   (D) so that

20. You look _______ you've seen a ghost.
   (A) so that
   (B) as long as
   (C) as if
   (D) until

21. I refuse to pay anything _______ you do the work properly.
   (A) while
   (B) as long as
   (C) so that
   (D) until

22. I'm going shopping for food this evening _______ I don't have to go at the weekend.
   (A) so that
   (B) as long as
   (C) while
   (D) until

23. You look _______ you haven't eaten for a week.
   (A) consequently
   (B) for
   (C) as though
   (D) until

24. I came early _______ I could talk to you privately.
   (A) so that
   (B) as long as
   (C) until
   (D) as if

25. _______ I don't think she's perfect for the job, she's certainly better qualified than Raj.

   (A) But
   (B) as long as
   (C) while
   (D) for

26. I don't mind if you go out for lunch _______ you would be back for the meeting at 2 pm.
   (a) as if
   (B) till
   (C) while
   (D) provided that

27. Are you OK? You look _______ you have a problem.
   (A) but
   (B) as though
   (C) as well as
   (D) until

28. _______ the job is very interesting, it's also very badly paid.
   (A) Although
   (B) till
   (C) since
   (D) until

29. We'll go to the mountains on Saturday _______ it doesn't rain.
   (A) before
   (B) as long as
   (C) if
   (D) that

30. Here the winters are very cold _______ the summers are very hot.
   (A) since
   (B) but
   (C) while
   (D) until

Read the passages below and select respective options that can correctly replace the underlined portions.

In the past, tigers were considered as pests. _______31_________ a smaller area to hunt, ______32_______ man had taken up more of the land to build upon, the tigers found less areas for themselves to hunt. They therefore turned to farms to get their food. Farmers' livestock were attacked by these tigers. People were then encouraged to kill the animals with the promise of rewards. ______33________ the threat of tigers on livestock was over, man continued to hunt tigers, now for recreation. Poachers knowing that the skin of tigers is much sought after ______34________, hunted tigers ______35_______ their body parts. Bones and other organs are both used as ingredients in traditional Chinese medicine.

31.
(A) For	(B) When
(C) With	(D) Yet

32.
(A) till	(B) for
(C) Until	(D) when

33.
(A) Even if	(B) Since
(C) Despite	(D) Even after

34.
(A) and	(B) too
(C) But	(D) since

35.
(A) not only	(B) both
(C) For	(D) also

OLYMPIAD WORKBOOK (IEO) CLASS— 9

—Darken Your Choice with HB Pencil—

1. Ⓐ Ⓑ Ⓒ Ⓓ	8. Ⓐ Ⓑ Ⓒ Ⓓ	15. Ⓐ Ⓑ Ⓒ Ⓓ	22. Ⓐ Ⓑ Ⓒ Ⓓ	29. Ⓐ Ⓑ Ⓒ Ⓓ
2. Ⓐ Ⓑ Ⓒ Ⓓ	9. Ⓐ Ⓑ Ⓒ Ⓓ	16. Ⓐ Ⓑ Ⓒ Ⓓ	23. Ⓐ Ⓑ Ⓒ Ⓓ	30. Ⓐ Ⓑ Ⓒ Ⓓ
3. Ⓐ Ⓑ Ⓒ Ⓓ	10. Ⓐ Ⓑ Ⓒ Ⓓ	17. Ⓐ Ⓑ Ⓒ Ⓓ	24. Ⓐ Ⓑ Ⓒ Ⓓ	31. Ⓐ Ⓑ Ⓒ Ⓓ
4. Ⓐ Ⓑ Ⓒ Ⓓ	11. Ⓐ Ⓑ Ⓒ Ⓓ	18. Ⓐ Ⓑ Ⓒ Ⓓ	25. Ⓐ Ⓑ Ⓒ Ⓓ	32. Ⓐ Ⓑ Ⓒ Ⓓ
5. Ⓐ Ⓑ Ⓒ Ⓓ	12. Ⓐ Ⓑ Ⓒ Ⓓ	19. Ⓐ Ⓑ Ⓒ Ⓓ	26. Ⓐ Ⓑ Ⓒ Ⓓ	33. Ⓐ Ⓑ Ⓒ Ⓓ
6. Ⓐ Ⓑ Ⓒ Ⓓ	13. Ⓐ Ⓑ Ⓒ Ⓓ	20. Ⓐ Ⓑ Ⓒ Ⓓ	27. Ⓐ Ⓑ Ⓒ Ⓓ	34. Ⓐ Ⓑ Ⓒ Ⓓ
7. Ⓐ Ⓑ Ⓒ Ⓓ	14. Ⓐ Ⓑ Ⓒ Ⓓ	21. Ⓐ Ⓑ Ⓒ Ⓓ	28. Ⓐ Ⓑ Ⓒ Ⓓ	35. Ⓐ Ⓑ Ⓒ Ⓓ

MODEL TEST PAPER

WORD & STRUCTURE KNOWLEDGE

Choose the right word/phrase that completes the sentence.

1. I ______ confess I don't think much of his new hairstyle.
    (A) will (B) should
    (C) ought to (D) must

2. 'Honda factories ______ as supplier strike continues'.
    (A) paralyzed (B) grounded
    (C) halted (D) obstructed

3. My brother works in a large office ______ I work from home.
    (A) nevertheless (B) however
    (C) whereas (D) although

4. That is a very______ excuse. I don't believe it.
    (A) poor (B) false
    (C) lame (D) phoney

5. Sara's a bit of ______, isn't she? Who would have thought she'd write a best-selling novel?
    (A) a soft touch
    (B) a dark horse
    (C) a rough diamond
    (D) a snake in the grass

6. Does Vivek have the necessary ______ to be called for the interview?
    (A) skills (B) abilities
    (C) references (D) qualifications

7. I hope I didn't ______ you any trouble by coming without calling first.
    (A) create (B) make
    (C) cause (D) bring

8. Dear Mr. Rao, Thank you for your support. ______ sincerely, Ritu Pandey.
    (A) Your (B) You're
    (C) Your's (D) Yours

9. Would you ______ some medium-sized onions from that pile over there?
    (A) pick up (B) pick out
    (C) pick over (D) pick through

10. I worked as a waiter for a year, but it was the tips that were my real ______.
    (A) milk and honey
    (B) sugar and spice
    (C) bread and butter
    (D) peaches and cream

11. That new restaurant down the road has great seafood and some absolutely ______ desserts.
    (A) iresistable (B) iresistible
    (C) irresistible (D) irresistable

12. Choose the word/phrase which explains the meaning of the underlined word.

    Did you get what the teacher was saying?
    (A) know (B) receive
    (C) recognize (D) understand

13. Which of the following does NOT take tele- as a prefix?
    (A) -scope (B) -sonic
    (C) -vision (D) -graphy

Choose the odd one out from each set.

14. (A) sniff (B) snicker
    (C) giggle (D) chuckle

15. (A) warm: quilt
    (B) spiny: porcupine
    (C) sandy: beach
    (D) page: book

GRAMMAR

Fill in the blanks with the correct word/ phrase.

16. As soon as I arrived, we _____ our food – everyone had waited for me.
    (A) were ordering   (B) ordered
    (C) had ordered   (D) would order

17. Anil: I went to see Three Idiots yesterday. It's excellent.
    Balu: Oh good. I am seeing it tomorrow.
    Anil: I know you _____ it.
    (A) will love   (B) going to love
    (C) shall love   (D) love

18. I _____ if I had their lifestyle!
    (A) would not have complained
    (B) would not complain
    (C) will not complain
    (D) did not complain

19. Would you mind _____ the music down? I can't concentrate.
    (A) turn   (B) to turn
    (C) turning   (D) to turning

Choose the part of the sentence that contains an error. If there is no error, choose D.

20. (A) We haven't got / (b) many homeworks / (c) this week. / (d) No error

21. (A) They said / (b) they'd phone us / (c) until their plane lands. / (d) No error

22. (A) Most of the pollution / (b) in city centres / (c) is caused by fuel emissions. / (d) No error

Given below are sets of two sentences. Both sentences may be right or both wrong or one of thetwo may be right. Select the correct option.

23. P: She wasn't at work yesterday because she had to go to hospital for an appointment.
    Q: I'm not going to play golf today as I had good game yesterday.
    (A) both right   (B) both wrong
    (C) only P right   (D) only Q right

24. P: His application for admission to engineering, that was received yesterday, has gonemissing.
    Q: The bouquet of flowers, which was ordered yesterday, has just arrived.
    (A) both right   (B) both wrong
    (C) only P right   (D) only Q right

25. P: I think it is a good idea to ban autos from the city centre.
    Q: You need to realize that to save a rupee is to earn a rupee.
    (A) both right   (B) both wrong
    (C) only P right   (D) only Q right

READING

World Sports Meet 2011

THIRD DAY'S SCHEDULE

SHOOTING

- Pairs 25 m Pistol Women
- Stage 1 (Precision and Rapid)
- Pairs 10 m Air Rifle Men's Final
- Pairs 50 m Pistol Men's Final
- Pairs 50 m Rifle 3 positions Women's Final

Starts at 9 a.m.

CYCLING

- 500 m Time Trial Women's Finals
- 1000 m Time Trial Men's Finals
- Individual Pursuit Men's Finals

Starts at 1.30 p.m.

ARTISTIC GYMNASTICS

- Team Final and Individual Qualification Women

Starts at 1.30 p.m.

WEIGHTLIFTING
- 62 kg Men's Finals
- 53 kg Women's Finals

Starts at 2 p.m.

SWIMMING
- 50 m Butterfly Women's Finals
- 50 m Backstroke Men's Finals
- 50 m Breaststroke Women's Finals
- 50 m Freestyle Women's Finals
- 200 m Freestyle Men's Finals

Starts at 4 p.m.

WRESTLING
- 66 kg Freestyle Men's Finals
- 74 kg Freestyle Men's Finals
- 96 kg Freestyle Men's Finals

Starts at 4.30 p.m.

26. What time does the 50 m Breaststroke Women's Finals start?

    (A) 9 a.m.   (B) 1.30 p.m.
    (C) 4 p.m.   (D) 4.30 p.m.

27. How many sports events start at 1.30 p.m. ?

    (A) 1   (B) 2
    (C) 3   (D) 4

28. The event '53 kg Women's Finals' refers to:

    (A) Weightlifting
    (B) Wrestling
    (C) Artistic gymnastics
    (D) Swimming

29. Sushil Kumar, the wrestling champion, is participating in the 66 kg Men's Freestyle Finals on thethird day of the Commonwealth Games. At what time can you see him on TV?

    (A) Before 4.30 p.m.
    (B) At 4.30 p.m.
    (C) From 4.30 p.m.
    (D) Sometime after 4.30 p.m.

PASSAGE 2

Orang-utans "require less food than humans, pound-for-pound," lead author Herman Pontzer said.

When they do eat orang-utans nibble mostly on ripe fruit, along with smaller portions of leaves andseed. Even in captivity, this diet doesn't diminish an orang-utan's get-up-and-go. "They wake up early,after a long night's sleep," explained Pontzer, an assistant professor of anthropology at WashingtonUniversity in St. Louis. "Then they spend the day socializing, exploring their indoor or outdoorenclosures. They also regularly engage in games with researchers".

According to a study, published in the latest Proceedings of the National Academy of Sciences, theseactivities of the orangutan's, taken together add up to the same level of exercise performed byhumans in physically demanding agricultural lifestyles.

In the wild, orang-utans live in the rainforests of Borneo and Sumatra where food availability is highlyvariable and unpredictable, Pontzer added. Like fresh fruit from the garden, the pickings are oftenfeast or famine. "But the trade-off," he added, "is that low-energy throughout means less energy isavailable to do things like grow and reproduce. So orang-utans grow slowly and reproduce slowly,which is evolutionarily risky because an orang-utan might die before it passes on its genes." Humanmothers can have a child every two to four years, but orang-utans in the wild only reproduce everyseven to eight years.

Orang-utans are highly endangered, with many lost due to human activities such as logging, miningand the illegal pet trade. Pontzer hopes the study will highlight "how much information we lose aboutour closest relatives and our own evolutionary history if we let them go extinct."

30. Orang-utans eat _____ humans do.
    (A) less than
    (B) more than
    (C) the same amount as
    (D) nearly as much as
31. According to Pontzer, orang-utans are
    (A) lazy.   (B) friendly.
    (C) slow.   (D) energetic.
32. According to the study published in the Proceedings of the National Academy of Sciences,
    (A) orang-utans and farmers do the same amount of physical activity.
    (B) orang-utans do the same exercises as farmers.
    (C) orang-utans and farmers work very hard.
    (D) orang-utans and farmers have similar lifestyles.
33. Orang-utans grow slowly and reproduce slowly because they
    (A) don't get sufficient food.
    (B) don't get fresh fruit from the garden.
    (C) eat low energy food.
    (D) don't eat enoughfood.
34. Pontzer does not want the orang-utans to become extinct because
    (A) they are our closest relatives.
    (B) they are an endangered species.
    (C) a lot of information about our evolution will be lost.
    (D) he wishes to study them in the wild.
35. Select the statement that is NOT TRUE.
    (A) The orang-utan reproductive cycle is slow.
    (B) Orang-utans have low energy levels.
    (C) All orang-utans may not reproduce.
    (D) Orang-utans give birth every four years.

PASSAGE 3

"Most of my time is spent in my room, French-plaiting other girls' hair," said Rachael Burford, centreplayer in the England women's rugby team. Burford, and her braided friends then go out on the rugbypitch where, if you caught any of the recent World Cup, you will have noticed that the women are justas fearless as their male counterparts. "It has got to the point now when I feel a bit weird if I don't do someone's hair before a game," saidBurford. "Some of the girls look really tough with their hair plaited, so it's also a psychological thing —a victorious thing." Sadly, victory wasn't tied up in those braids — the team lost to New Zealand in theSeptember 5 final — but many of the players looked fierce, like warrior women going into battle."Plaits are the earliest of hairstyles because before haircutting and hairdressing, people obviously hadlong hair and plaits were the simplest way of keeping it out of the way," says fashion historian CarolineCox. For that reason, she says, we associate plaits with both women and men, and particularly thosewho are involved in athletic pursuits, such as war. Think of Legolas in "The Lord of the Rings", or thesuper strong Obelix in the "Asterix" cartoons. "For women, Boudicca or Valkyrie plaits seem toenhance their ferocity," says Cox.

"It was a practical hairstyle until we get to the 19th century, when it begins to be associated withfemale children. Even now, plaits on the whole have the meaning of the youthful schoolgirl." Not animage you will associate with England's nearly victorious rugby team.

36. Rachel Burford is a
    (A) central player.   (B) hairdresser.
    (C) rugby player.   (D) fearless fighter.
37. During the World Cup, all her hair plaited friends
    (A) played fearlessly.
    (B) were able to beat male players.
    (C) won the World Cup.
    (D) were well appreciated.
38. Burford feels that whenever she plaits her friends' hair, they will _____ the match.
    (A) win   (B) lose
    (C) draw   (D) play

39. In paragraph 2, the phrase 'a psychological thing' refers to
    (A) plaiting her friends' hair.
    (B) feeling confident with plaited hair.
    (C) playing a mind game.
    (D) Burford's feeling of weirdness.

40. According to the passage, which of these statements is true?
    (A) Modern athletes plait their hair.
    (B) Both men and women used to plait their hair in olden days.
    (C) Plaiting and victory are synonymous in athletics.
    (D) Plaiting was a convenient hairstyle for athletes.

SPOKEN AND WRITTEN EXPRESSIONS

Spoken Expression

Choose the most suitable option to complete the dialogue.

41. Ram: Good morning. Is that Biz Comp?

    Uma: Good morning. This is Biz Comp. How can I help you?

    Ram: I am Ram Kerkar from Minerva Computers. I'd like to speak to Ms. Piali Ghosh, Head, HR.

    Uma: ________________________

    (A) Sorry. Ms. Ghosh is not here. You can talk to Mr. Naik of the computer section, if you like.
    (B) Sorry, Mr. Ram. Ms. Ghosh is not here at present. I'm her secretary. You can tell me what you want.
    (C) I'm sorry, Mr. Kerkar, but Ms. Ghosh is away this week. Would you like to leave a message?
    (D) I'm sorry, Mr. Kerkar. You can't speak to her. She's not here. You can speak to me. I'm her secretary.

42. Principal: Mr. D'Souza, the Annual Day's coming up. I've been wondering whom to invite as our chief guest this year. Do you have any suggestions?

Teacher: ________________________
    (A) Who? Me? I haven't a clue. How would I know anybody important enough?
    (B) Well, I don't really know anyone. But I can find out. I'll ask Mrs Sharma.
    (C) Why are you making such a fuss, sir? You'll find someone. You know so many important people.
    (D) Oh, there must be lots of people simply dying to be asked. Should be no problem at all.

43. Mrs K: Hello, Nita.

    Nita: Hello, Mrs Kumar. How have you been?

    Mrs K: Good. By the way, Nita, I'm having a party for my brother, Arun – the one who's come from the States. It's on Sunday. I'd like you to come.

    Nita: ________________________
    (A) Where's it going to be? Who else is coming? And how many people are you asking?
    (B) Ooh! That hunk! As handsome as ever, I'll bet. No way I'm going to miss it.
    (C) Sure. I love parties. Parties mean food. Hope there'll be lots of it.
    (D) Sure, I'll be there. Arun's back, is he? It'll be nice to see him again.

44. Ali: Pia, have you seen the ad? They're looking for a new editor. For the School Magazine. It's on the notice board. Why don't you apply?

    Pia: ________________________
    (A) Why should I? They're not going to get anyone like me. Let them come to me.
    (B) I don't think I will. Being an editor is tough – takes time and energy. Not sure I can spare that right now.
    (C) You bet, I will. You're not the first, you know. Everyone, including the teachers, has been asking me to apply.
    (D) I am afraid not. I do not deem this an appropriate moment to take on such an onerous responsibility.

45. Ali: Oh, well If that's how you feel… I just thought you were so right for the job.

Alan: There's a plan to get a film personality to be the face of our campaign tosave trees.

Bani: Why should we see actors as youth icons? After all, what do they have torecommend themselves?

Alan: ________________________________

(A) Whether you like it or not, actors have great influence on the youth. They imitate their heroes.

(B) Well, actors are usually good-looking. They're attractive and the youthtend to copy their dress and mannerisms.

(C) Actors? What do they know about trees and environment? All they have istheir looks and clothes.

(D) I think actors have a bad influence on youth and turn them into unthinking, mindless sheep.

Written Expression

Given below are four sentence paragraphs (S1-S4). S1 and S4 are given. From the options, (P, Q, R)choose two sentences for S2 and S3.

46. S1. Shops and homes in select areas of Maharashtra will soon have to pay in advance forthe electricity they use.

P. This follows the Maharashtra Electricity Board's approval for introducing prepaidmeters.

Q. The state's electricity distribution company will install 25,000 prepaid meters tobegin with.

R. The electricity meters will be installed free of cost in those shops and residences where usage is low.

S4. Customers using these meters will have to buy electricity using a card which can berecharged when the meter shows low credit

(A) QP   (B) PQ

(C) RQ   (D) QR

47. S1. The smoke of a devastating forest fire always carries two compounds, with it, a lifepromoter, and a regulator.

P. The forest fires have a role to play in maintaining a balance in nature.

Q. After forest fires have been extinguished, the seeds that abound on forestfloors take over to repopulate the burnt forest.

R. The regulatory chemical in the smoke keeps a check on these seeds and lets themgerminate only when there is enough moisture in the atmosphere again.

S4. Once the seeds have germinated the promoter chemical takes over to ensure a rapidre-growth of the forest.

(A) PQ   (B) QR

(C) RQ   (D) QP

48. S1. How the foot lands when one is running has a long evolutionary history.

P. Humans ran even when there were no shoes, for food, from predators, fires, andstorms.

Q. Natural selection ensured that barefoot runners landed on their forefoot whilerunning.

R. Running in a way that reduced the chances of foot injury to a minimum wasessential.

S4. Shod runners on the other hand land on their heels and need well cushioned shoes toabsorb the impact.

(A) RQ   (B) PQ

(C) QP   (D) QR

49. S1. You are invited to a learning opportunity at Kheladhri school.

P. We strive to cultivate the child's natural intelligence while building academic-excellence and physical fitness.

Q. The wider intent is to discover right living and right relationship with the earth.

R. Parents who wish to admit their children may write to us in December.

S4. Kheladhri is a fully residential school and is situated amidst great natural beauty in the Western Ghats, in India.

(A) RQ   (B) PR
(C) QP   (D) PQ

50. S1. Rag picking is not a new profession in India.

P. They are not, however, offered any constructive support by the local government.

Q. Every Indian city has had its own band of pickers for many years.

R. They keep the city clean, unofficially joining forces with the municipal staff

S4. They often work in dirty and hazardous conditions, but get no kudos for theseservices.

(A) QR   (B) RP
(C) QP   (D) PR

Darken Your Choice with HB Pencil

1. Ⓐ Ⓑ Ⓒ Ⓓ	11. Ⓐ Ⓑ Ⓒ Ⓓ	21. Ⓐ Ⓑ Ⓒ Ⓓ	31. Ⓐ Ⓑ Ⓒ Ⓓ	41. Ⓐ Ⓑ Ⓒ Ⓓ
2. Ⓐ Ⓑ Ⓒ Ⓓ	12. Ⓐ Ⓑ Ⓒ Ⓓ	22. Ⓐ Ⓑ Ⓒ Ⓓ	32. Ⓐ Ⓑ Ⓒ Ⓓ	42. Ⓐ Ⓑ Ⓒ Ⓓ
3. Ⓐ Ⓑ Ⓒ Ⓓ	13. Ⓐ Ⓑ Ⓒ Ⓓ	23. Ⓐ Ⓑ Ⓒ Ⓓ	33. Ⓐ Ⓑ Ⓒ Ⓓ	43. Ⓐ Ⓑ Ⓒ Ⓓ
4. Ⓐ Ⓑ Ⓒ Ⓓ	14. Ⓐ Ⓑ Ⓒ Ⓓ	24. Ⓐ Ⓑ Ⓒ Ⓓ	34. Ⓐ Ⓑ Ⓒ Ⓓ	44. Ⓐ Ⓑ Ⓒ Ⓓ
5. Ⓐ Ⓑ Ⓒ Ⓓ	15. Ⓐ Ⓑ Ⓒ Ⓓ	25. Ⓐ Ⓑ Ⓒ Ⓓ	35. Ⓐ Ⓑ Ⓒ Ⓓ	45. Ⓐ Ⓑ Ⓒ Ⓓ
6. Ⓐ Ⓑ Ⓒ Ⓓ	16. Ⓐ Ⓑ Ⓒ Ⓓ	26. Ⓐ Ⓑ Ⓒ Ⓓ	36. Ⓐ Ⓑ Ⓒ Ⓓ	46. Ⓐ Ⓑ Ⓒ Ⓓ
7. Ⓐ Ⓑ Ⓒ Ⓓ	17. Ⓐ Ⓑ Ⓒ Ⓓ	27. Ⓐ Ⓑ Ⓒ Ⓓ	37. Ⓐ Ⓑ Ⓒ Ⓓ	47. Ⓐ Ⓑ Ⓒ Ⓓ
8. Ⓐ Ⓑ Ⓒ Ⓓ	18. Ⓐ Ⓑ Ⓒ Ⓓ	28. Ⓐ Ⓑ Ⓒ Ⓓ	38. Ⓐ Ⓑ Ⓒ Ⓓ	48. Ⓐ Ⓑ Ⓒ Ⓓ
9. Ⓐ Ⓑ Ⓒ Ⓓ	19. Ⓐ Ⓑ Ⓒ Ⓓ	29. Ⓐ Ⓑ Ⓒ Ⓓ	39. Ⓐ Ⓑ Ⓒ Ⓓ	49. Ⓐ Ⓑ Ⓒ Ⓓ
10. Ⓐ Ⓑ Ⓒ Ⓓ	20. Ⓐ Ⓑ Ⓒ Ⓓ	30. Ⓐ Ⓑ Ⓒ Ⓓ	40. Ⓐ Ⓑ Ⓒ Ⓓ	50. Ⓐ Ⓑ Ⓒ Ⓓ

HINTS AND SOLUTIONS

1. SYNONYMS, ANTONYMS, HOMOPHONES AND HOMONYMS

Answer Key

1. (B)	2. (A)	3. (C)	4. (C)	5. (A)	6. (B)	7. (B)	8. (C)	9. (A)	10. (C)
11. (D)	12. (C)	13. (A)	14. (D)	15. (A)	16. (C)	17. (D)	18. (D)	19. (B)	20. (C)
21. (D)	22. (B)	23. (A)	24. (D)	25. (D)	26. (B)	27. (D)	28. (D)	29. (C)	30. (C)

HOTS (ACHIEVERS SECTION)

31. (B)	32. (B)	33. (D)	34. (D)	35. (A)

2. SPELLING, COLLOCATIONS AND JUMBLED WORDS

Answer Key

1. (A)	2. (A)	3. (B)	4. (A)	5. (B)	6. (A)	7. (B)	8. (A)	9. (A)	10. (B)
11. (B)	12. (A)	13. (B)	14. (A)	15. (A)	16. (B)	17. (A)	18. (B)	19. (B)	20. (A)
21. (D)	22. (D)	23. (D)	24. (C)	25. (C)	26. (B)	27. (B)	28. (A)	29. (C)	30. (B)

HOTS (ACHIEVERS SECTION)

31. (B)	32. (A)	33. (A)	34. (B)	35. (A)

3. ANALOGY AND ONE WORD

Answer Key

1. (C)	2. (C)	3. (C)	4. (B)	5. (C)	6. (C)	7. (A)	8. (C)	9. (C)	10. (B)
11. (F)	12. (T)	13. (T)	14. (T)	15. (F)	16. (A)	17. (A)	18. (C)	19. (B)	20. (A)
21. (B)	22. (B)	23. (A)	24. (C)	25. (A)	26. (B)	27. (A)	28. (B)	29. (A)	30. (C)

HOTS (ACHIEVERS SECTION)

31. (C)	32. (A)	33. (D)	34. (D)	35. (D)

4. PHRASAL VERBS AND IDIOMS

Answer Key

1. (B)	2. (A)	3. (D)	4. (C)	5. (B)	6. (D)	7. (B)	8. (C)	9. (D)	10. (B)
11. (D)	12. (A)	13. (B)	14. (D)	15. (C)	16. (A)	17. (A)	18. (C)	19. (C)	20. (D)
21. (D)	22. (A)	23. (B)	24. (A)	25. (D)					

26. look up	27. get on	28. turn on	29. give up	30. take off

HOTS (ACHIEVERS SECTION)

31. (B)	32. (A)	33. (C)	34. (A)	35. (A)

5. QUESTION FORMS

Answer Key

1. Yes/no	2. Choice
3. Yes/no	4. Question/word
5. Question/word	6. Question/word
7. Choice	8. Question/word
9. Question/word	10. Opinion
11. What is she opening?	12. Where are the boys hiding?
13. Who prefers porridge for breakfast?	14. What does Prasad have on Thursday?
15. When did Anil and Anu go to the swimming pool?	16. Where is the plane landing?
17. What is ringing?	18. Why does Chitra have to stop?
19. What is the cost of Ashima's new bike?	20. Who is walking along the beach?

HOTS (ACHIEVERS SECTION)

21. What does your brother like/love for dessert?
22. When is Prateek going for a movie?
23. Where did Anil and Anu leave for yesterday?

24. (B)	25. (A)

6. VERBS, ADVERBS AND CONCORD

Answer Key

1. (B)	2. (D)	3. (C)	4. (A)	5. (A)	6. (B)	7. (B)	8. (A)	9. (C)	10. (D)
11. (D)	12. (C)	13. (D)	14. (D)	15. (B)	16. (D)	17. (D)	18. (D)	19. (D)	20. (D)
21. (B)	22. (D)	23. (A)	24. (D)	25. (B)	26. (A)	27. (C)	28. (A)	29. (B)	30. (B)

31. (B)	32. (A)	33. (C)	34. (B)	35. (C)

7. NOUNS AND PRONOUNS

Answer Key

1. (C)	2. (A)	3. (D)	4. (B)	5. (D)	6. (C)	7. (A)	8. (B)	9. (A)	10. (C)
11. (C)	12. (A)	13. (D)	14. (D)	15. (C)	16. (B)	17. (C)	18. (C)	19. (A)	20. (B)
21. (A)	22. (A)	23. (C)	24. (C)	25. (B)	26. (B)	27. (C)	28. (D)	29. (A)	30. (B)

HOTS (ACHIEVERS SECTION)

31. (B)	32. (B)	33. (B)	34. (A)	35. (B)

8. ADJECTIVES

Answer Key

1. (B)	2. (A)	3. (A)	4. (C)	5. (C)	6. (A)	7. (A)	8. (A)	9. (B)	10. (A)
11. (B)	12. (A)	13. (A)	14. (D)	15. (B)	16. (A)	17. (C)	18. (B)	19. (D)	20. (C)
21. (A)	22. (D)	23. (D)	24. (D)	25. (A)					

HOTS (ACHIEVERS SECTION)

26. (C)	27. (C)	28. (A)	29. (C)	30. (A)

9. ARTICLES AND PREPOSITIONS

Answer Key

1. (B)	2. (B)	3. (A)	4. (A)	5. (B)	6. (A)	7. (A)	8. (B)	9. (A)	
10. a, an		11. a, the		12. an		13. an, a, the		14. an	
15. a, an		16. an		17. a, an, the		18. a		19. a, the	
20. x, a, a, an		21. an, a,x		22. a, an		23. a, a		24. an, a, a, x, a	
25. a, an		26. an, an		27. a, an		28. a, an		29. an, the	
30. a, an, x									

31. (B)	32. (A)	33. (C)	34. (B)	35. (A)

10. CONJUNCTION AND DETERMINERS

Answer Key

1. (C)	2. (D)	3. (C)	4. (C)	5. (C)	6. (D)	7. (A)	8. (B)	9. (A)	10. (B)
11. (A)	12. (D)	13. (B)	14. (C)	15. (A)	16. (A)	17. (B)	18. (C)	19. (A)	20. (C)

HOTS (ACHIEVERS SECTION)

21. (C)	22. (D)	23. (D)	24. (B)	25. (C)

1. **(C)**
   'A smaller area' is a contributing factor for the tigers to attack man and his livestock. Hence, 'with'.

4. **(B)**
   An additional conjunction is needed. 'Too' is correct.

5. **(C)**
   The purpose why poachers hunt is to get their body parts. Hence "for".

11. SENTENCE SEQUENCING

Answer Key

1. (B)	2. (B)	3. (A)	4. (A)	5. (B)	6. (A)	7. (B)	8. (D)	9. (B)	10. (B)
11. (D)	12. (A)	13. (B)	14. (C)	15. (C)	16. (B)	17. (D)	18. (B)	19. (A)	20. (C)

HOTS (ACHIEVERS SECTION)

21. (B)	22. (D)	23. (A)	24. (B)	25. (D)

12. TENSES AND CONDITIONALS

Answer Key

1. (D)	2. (A)	3. (D)	4. (C)	5. (B)	6. (C)	7. (D)	8. (B)	9. (A)	10. (B)
11. (D)	12. (B)	13. (C)	14. (B)	15. (A)	16. (B)	17. (D)	18. (D)	19. (D)	20. (C)
21. (C)	22. (A)	23. (A)	24. (B)	25. (C)	26. (D)	27. (A)	28. (D)	29. (A)	30. (C)

31. is going	32. is carrying	33. is	34. puts, is wearing	35. is taking, is raining

13. VOICE AND NARRATION

Answer Key

1. (B)	2. (B)	3. (B)	4. (B)	5. (A)	6. (B)	7. (C)	8. (B)	9. (A)	10. (A)
11. (C)	12. (C)	13. (D)	14. (C)	15. (B)	16. (B)	17. (A)	18. (A)	19. (A)	20. (D)
21. (A)	22. (C)	23. (B)	24. (B)	25. (A)	26. (D)	27. (D)	28. (D)	29. (D)	30. (B)

HOTS (ACHIEVERS SECTION)

31. I was eaten an ice cream.	32. He was written a novel.

14. COMPREHENSION

Answer Key

I.	1. (c)	2. (a)	3. (c)	4. (d)	5. (c)
II.	6. Dictionary	7. Pronunciation	8. Different fields have different definitions for the same term	9. Nimbus	

III.

10. Computers are taking over. Typing is considered as good as typing.
11. Because she was used to writing on the laptop and she had no cursive writing practice.
12. Cursive writing was originally developed to make it easier for children to write with a pen.
13. It is a better way to store written language skills in a child's brain than pressing keys.
14. When children keep their devices, it sets up the bad habit of neglecting to write.
15. It shows that in the future sending a handwritten letter will be a display of wealth and class.
16. they interrupt writing practice/ stay with their devices.
17. learning to type.

IV.

18.
(A) The level of a persons self-confidence and enthusiasm at a particular time.
(B) Comfort or sympathise somebody who is unhappy or disappointed.
(C) Lack of something.

19.
(A) The other long-distance sailors had learnt that the single-hander's main enemies were lacking of confidence, having discouragement and loneliness. This was discovered by Ann Davison.
(B) One learns from the passage that sailing was a passion for Ann. But, since her boat was not working properly, she had decided to sail a little everyday. This would help her not to lose her confidence

and keep her motivated. Hence, I think, the author says, "It was good for her morale".

(C) When a squall struck her boat, Ann gave up trying to sail and consoled herself by reading poetry in the cabin.

(D) Ann was suffering from fatigue which she suspected was as a result of a vitamin deficiency. Therefore, owing to her deteriorating physical health and mental depression, she decided to head for Barbados instead of Antigua, as it was nearer.

(E) For steering better, Ann tried to stream heavy ropes backwards. But, due to the changing directions of the violent wind, the ropes got tangled up and she had to pull them to the cockpit to untangle them. This exhausted her even more.

20.

Ann Davison was a very courageous woman with strong determination. The gift pack by her friends made her feel lonely. This shows that she was emotional too. The sudden strong and violent winds stopped her for a while but could not discourage her. Instead of being demoralised, she busied herself in reading and playing memory games. This shows her self-motivation. Deficiency of fuel and deteriorating health disheartened her a little but could not deviate her from reaching her goal.

15. SPOKEN AND WRITTEN EXPRESSIONS; PUNCTUATION

Answer Key

1. (A)	2. (B)	3. (B)	4. (C)	5. (B)	6. (C)	7. (A)	8. (B)	9. (A)	10. (C)
11. (A)	12. (C)	13. (C)	14. (B)	15. (C)	16. (B)	17. (C)	18. (A)	19. (C)	20. (C)
21. (D)	22. (A)	23. (C)	24. (A)	25. (C)	26. (D)	27. (B)	28. (A)	29. (B)	30. (C)

HOTS (ACHIEVERS SECTION)

31. (C)	32. (D)	33. (D)	34. (B)	35. (C)

MODEL TEST PAPER

Answer Key

1. (D)	2. (A)	3. (C)	4. (C)	5. (B)	6. (D)	7. (C)	8. (D)	9. (B)	10. (C)
11. (C)	12. (D)	13. (B)	14. (A)	15. (D)	16. (B)	17. (A)	18. (B)	19. (C)	20. (B)
21. (C)	22. (D)	23. (B)	24. (D)	25. (A)	26. (C)	27. (D)	28. (A)	29. (A)	30. (A)
31. (B)	32. (A)	33. (A)	34. (C)	35. (D)	36. (C)	37. (A)	38. (A)	39. (A)	40. (B)
41. (C)	42. (B)	43. (D)	44. (B)	45. (B)	46. (B)	47. (B)	48. (A)	49. (D)	50. (A)

SAMPLE OMR ANSWER SHEET

1. STUDENT NAME (IN ENGLISH CAPITAL LETTERS ONLY)

Students must write and darken the respective circles completely using HB Pencil only. Othewise their Answer Sheets will not be evaluated.

PERSONAL DETAILS

2. SCHOOL CODE

3. CLASS

4. SECTION

5. ROLL NO.

6. QUESTION PAPER SET

A ○
B ○
C ○
D ○

7. MOBILE NUMBER

8. GENDER

MALE ○
FEMALE ○

9. STREAM
(Only for Class XI and XII Students)

MATHEMATICS ○
BIOLOGY ○
OTHERS ○

MARK YOUR ANSWERS

1.	A	B	C	D	26.	A	B	C	D
2.	A	B	C	D	27.	A	B	C	D
3.	A	B	C	D	28.	A	B	C	D
4.	A	B	C	D	29.	A	B	C	D
5.	A	B	C	D	30.	A	B	C	D
6.	A	B	C	D	31.	A	B	C	D
7.	A	B	C	D	32.	A	B	C	D
8.	A	B	C	D	33.	A	B	C	D
9.	A	B	C	D	34.	A	B	C	D
10.	A	B	C	D	35.	A	B	C	D
11.	A	B	C	D	36.	A	B	C	D
12.	A	B	C	D	37.	A	B	C	D
13.	A	B	C	D	38.	A	B	C	D
14.	A	B	C	D	39.	A	B	C	D
15.	A	B	C	D	40.	A	B	C	D
16.	A	B	C	D	41.	A	B	C	D
17.	A	B	C	D	42.	A	B	C	D
18.	A	B	C	D	43.	A	B	C	D
19.	A	B	C	D	44.	A	B	C	D
20.	A	B	C	D	45.	A	B	C	D
21.	A	B	C	D	46.	A	B	C	D
22.	A	B	C	D	47.	A	B	C	D
23.	A	B	C	D	48.	A	B	C	D
24.	A	B	C	D	49.	A	B	C	D
25.	A	B	C	D	50.	A	B	C	D

Signature of the Student & Date of Examination

Signature of the Invigilator & Date of Examination